Endorsements

A Paradigm Shift of Prophetic Revelation is an exceptional writing that has much-needed scriptural content to assist us in the course of maturing into the prophetic lifestyle. Rich Harris has captured a revelatory dimension that teaches from a simple practicality to a depth that walks us from the origin of prophecy to today's modern times without omitting any of God's principles.

Prophet Jimmie Reed
Revelation International

I have had the privilege of knowing Rich Harris for nearly seven years. During this time, I became a spiritual son of his, truly seeing the character of the man behind closed doors. To say that Rich puts more focus on the character of the prophetic person without cutting short the process of maturity would be an understatement! *A Paradigm Shift of Prophetic Revelation* is a great step-by-step book that not only puts the proper emphasis on the process we must go through to be more than just a shooting star. Rich does an amazing job of clearly explaining the function and purpose of prophetic people and the New Covenant prophet. In today's church world, there are many so-called prophetic voices and yet so few words seem to be landing and accomplishing the will of God. Everyone should read this book!

Justin Carpenter
Cross Kingdom Ministries Kerrville, TX

Rich Harris has put into words the "aha" we all experience in failure and growth in the prophetic awareness. He speaks from a father's heart as a learner, teacher, and leader in the prophetic. He shows us that God tailor-made human life to speak through. Read, digest, and absorb this spiritual practical teaching. You will return to it again and again.

Val Rensink
Fort Mill, SC

Rich Harris has once again given us a gem of insight. Filled with personal examples and appropriate scriptural references, this book will lead anyone seeking an understanding of the prophetic on a journey that begins with basics and leads to maturity. Rich is a gifted teacher, and his ability to pass on truth is clearly demonstrated in this writing. This is a book you will refer to again and again for instruction and clarity in your own prophetic walk.

Apostle Wes Schoel
Jacksonville, FL

It is my honor to endorse *A Paradigm Shift of Prophetic Revelation*. Not only is Rich Harris my spiritual father in the prophetic realm, but he is a spiritual father to many others. In this book, he takes us on a journey of exploration, discovering, and revealing the heart of God not only in regard to prophetic ministry but in becoming a prophetic people as sons of God.

This book explores simple truths, takes us into practical aspects of receiving and releasing words of revelation, and reveals the realm of God's heart. In that place, we behold our heavenly Father and begin to become like Him, speaking His words from His heart of love.

In Rich's written work, you will also learn to navigate the pitfalls of the prophetic and war victoriously with your words of prophecy. The pages are filled with treasures and abound with nuggets of truth and anointing to impart the spirit of prophecy to those who read it with an open heart.

Whether you are just learning to hear God for yourself and are desiring to flow in the prophetic to bless others or are a church leader longing to develop a mature people in the things of the Spirit, this book is for you. Through the training, application, and impartation found in this writing, you will be well equipped to move with the Spirit of God in releasing what He is saying today.

Jeanie Richardson
Firepoint Church

A Paradigm Shift of Prophetic Revelation

by Rich Harris

Golden Eagle Publishing
11413 W I-70 Frontage Rd North
Wheat Ridge, CO 80033

Copyright © 2017 by Rich Harris

All rights reserved. No part of this publication may be reproduced or transmitted in any form or by any means electronic or mechanical, including photocopy, recording or any information storage and retrieval system, except in the case of brief quotations embodied in critical articles or reviews without written permission from the publisher.

All Scripture references, unless otherwise indicated, are from the *New King James Version* © 1982 Thomas Nelson, Inc. Used by permission.

Scripture quotations marked CJB are taken from the *Complete Jewish Bible* © 1998. Used by permission.

ISBN 978-0-9785398-3-2

Editing, interior and cover design by Lightning Tree Creative Media
Cover Photo by Susan Thomas - Robertson

Golden Eagle Publishing
A Division of
Living Word Ministries International
11413 W I-70 Frontage Rd North
Wheat Ridge, CO 80033
303.989.2208
www.livingwordevents.org

Printed in the United States of America

Dedication

I dedicate this book to all prophetic people who desire to know "what is the width and length and depth and height–to know the love of Christ which passes knowledge; that we may be filled with all the fullness of God" (Ephesians 3:18-19 paraphrased). For without this love the prophetic ministry is only making noise. May *A Paradigm Shift of Prophetic Revelation* advance the Church into the Kingdom of God.

Rich Harris, 2017

Clearly Hear His Voice

Rich
17 Dec, 2023

Contents

Prologue 11
Introduction 17
Chapter 1 - First Steps in a New Nature 21
   Becoming Childlike 21
   The Promise of Maturity and Transformation 23
   Moving Into His Nature 26
   Identity Theft 29
   Disciplines of Practice 33
   Humility 36
   Growing in the Word 36
Chapter 2 - Comprehending Prophecy 41
   A New Covenant 43
   Called Before Commissioned 46
   The Call of God 48
   In Good Company 49
   The Sons of the Prophets 50
   Coming to Maturity 52
   Beginning Words 54
   The Works of Prophecy 57
Chapter 3 - Knowing the True 61
   The Beginning 65
   Do Not Be Ignorant 66
   Advancing the Kingdom 69
   The Key of Love 70
   Dealing with False Prophecy 72
Chapter 4 - New Covenant Prophecy 77
   New Covenant Functions 79
   Three Categories of Prophecy 82
   The *Gift* of Prophecy 84
   Prophetic Ministry 85
   The Function of the Prophet 85
   The Importance of Biblical Standards 86

The Prophetic Minister 88
The Prophet Office 89
New Covenant Realities 91
Chapter 5- Contending for Victory 93
    Chasing That Which We Already Have 95
    The Turning 96
    Prophetic Merit of Victories 98
    The Battles of Israel 100
    King Jehoshaphat's Battle 101
    Elisha's Word and Jeroram's Assumption 103
    Warring Against Jezebel, Witchcraft, and Religious Spirit ... 104
    Prophecy and Spiritual Warfare 107
Chapter 6 - The Revelatory Gifts of the Spirit 111
    Discovering Revelatory Gifts 112
    Defining Revelatory Gifts 115
    The Ways God Speaks 118
    Anatomy of Prophetic Flow 121
    Releasing the Prophetic Word 122
Chapter 7 - Processing Pure Prophetic Words 125
    Spirit and Life 126
    The Process 130
    Love Is the Key 133
    Renewed Prophetic Words 134
Chapter 8 - Led by the Spirit of God 137
    Words of God's Intent and Purpose 140
    Determining Prophetic Truth 142
    Do Not Quench the Spirit 145
    The Need for Diplomacy 147
    Prophetic Administration 148
    Sons of God 150
Chapter 9 - Experiencing the Prophetic Realm 153
    Born Again 154
    A New Life 155
    Growing Pains 156

Personal Experiences 157
Voices, Visions, and Angels 158
UFO's in Roswell, New Mexico 166
Trance 167
Simple Words 170
Chapter 10 - Practicing Prophecy in the Church 173
Building Teams 174
Developing Prophetic Protocol 177
Concerning Prophetic Teams 180
Protocol for Visiting Prophetic Ministers 181
Practicing Prophecy 181
Practicing Words of Warning 187
Words Concerning Direction 189
What About Corrective Words? 191
Last Words 194
Books by Golden Eagle Ministries 196

A Paradigm Shift of Prophetic Revelation

Prologue

By Rev. Troy L. Harris

As we enter further into the first half of the 21st century, we find ourselves faced with new questions, new situations, and new concerns not only as a Church, but as individuals and societies. The world we live in seems in constant turmoil with so little that can be called sure, certain, and timeless. Our forefathers relied on certain bedrock principles to give them the kind of foundational certainty that helped them shape their times and guide their individual and corporate lives. Highest among those principles was the primary place of God and His Word in their lives, which they revered and sought daily for wisdom and direction.

In days not long passed, Christianity had a powerful presence in the world and was seen as the source of wisdom and guidance for the world. While that notion could not be seen as entirely universal, it did indeed make a difference to many. The Church mattered. Presidents, prime ministers, politicians, and kings sought out the Church's best and brightest leaders for counsel and the Bible was the best-selling book on the shelves. Children were taught not only the stories of the Bible, but its doctrines and even its remarkable wisdom, logic, and life-changing power. Prayer was in schools. Shops were closed on Sundays and traditional religious holidays. At bare minimum, living by the Ten Commandments was seen as the right way to live, often reduced to a summation, the Golden Rule, to love God and neighbour and was binding on all good citizens.

A Paradigm Shift of Prophetic Revelation

Today, we are faced with a world that has not only largely turned its back on God, but has even become hostile to Him and His Word. It is not uncommon to hear people today who proudly proclaim themselves free from religion or who perhaps claim a belief in God but live as though He is an afterthought, barely devoting an hour or two a week, if not much less, to serving Him. Attacking God and His people is so common today that such actions have become a lame cliché.

This turning away has manifested itself in many respects even in the Church. The Scriptures are often presented in a watered-down manner, sin is regarded as too confrontational to teach unless it is rebranded in a user-friendly fashion and Christianity is taught as a participation in a faith comprised of sound-bite sized beliefs and with a culture that ironically mirrors the consumer driven society in which it finds itself. This new brand of Christianity is to a large extent an attempt to engage with a world that has less time for study and prayer and more time for electronic social networking and entertainment. It presumes that people have a short attention span and to keep their attention, the church must use the tools of the world–it must be entertaining and not concerned with details to reach them through that worldly haze of attention deficit.

However, the Church does seem to be awakening to the fact that this recent approach simply doesn't work. The Church is, in fact, to an unhealthily large extent, becoming less relevant because it looks just like the world. There is simply not much contrast. The Church looks like it is merely selling another product—one which people without Christ deem themselves to already have—a set of beliefs relevant to their own opinions with no real challenge to change their lives other than superficially.

In fact, this novel and overly worldly process of doing church disarms the Church of its most potent weapon—the Spirit of God. Only the Spirit of God can make the beautiful kind of radical believer that turned the world around in the Church's infancy. The earliest Christians who preached Jesus to the world, even converting an entire Empire, taught and lived a faith that was empowered, emboldened, and driven by the Spirit's work in their midst. Their faith was uncompromising, even to the point of suffering and being seen as "holy fools." Yet their faith and love opened hardened pagan hearts to God, and their doctrine not only radically changed individual lives but entire nations, becoming the foundation of the best that civilization would ever have in its entire history.

But what was it that the Spirit did in those ancient believers that made the world take such notice? Surely other religions had zeal for their beliefs. Other religions also taught radical ways of life, or had outwardly compelling worship, and some religions that came after Christianity would also have these in their midst. After all, all religions have beliefs, prayers, worship, and zeal. What made Christianity different?

An ancient Christian teacher, Tertullian (AD 160-220) drew a contrast between Christians and pagans by the fact that Christians had a self-sacrificial love for each other. He testified that the Romans would exclaim of the Christians *"see how they love one another!"* Another early Christian, Justin Marytr (martyred ad 165), wrote, *"We used to hate and destroy one another and refused to associate with people of another race or country. Now, because of Christ, we live together with such people and pray for our enemies."* The early Christians radically loved, and their lives were so different to that of the world around them, which history shows they shunned at every point, that they were also seen as radically holy.

Love and holiness were the difference. This can only come about by the power of the Gospel, driven by the Spirit of God, creating new men and women, twice-born and filled with the Spirit, preaching a message of power and grace.

In this juncture in our history, Pastor Rich Harris' book is a timely call for a return to biblical, Spirit empowered Christianity. However, to truly understand Rich's message is to see his underlying plea for holiness. To bear true spiritual fruit, one must be a good tree. The use of spiritual gifts is no exception. The gifts and fruit of the Spirit are intended to be used by those who seek true holiness, having a close, intimate relationship with God, knowing His heart, Word, and intention. Holiness, with its humility, love, and reverence for God and His word is the centre of the Christian life, and without it not only will no one see the Lord, but there will be no peace in God's house (see Hebrews 12:14). A cow goes "moo" because it is a cow. One cannot assume that by making a sound like a "moo" one would become a cow. Likewise, the fruits and gifts of the Spirit are not forthcoming or effective by imitation or merely seeking after them, however fervently, but they are true, genuine and effective when operated by truly spiritual people—the holy people of God called to use them as the Spirit has gifted them, for His purpose.

Pastor Rich's book here presented is an earnest plea for holiness of heart and life, for a deeper fellowship with God to know Him and His purpose in order to make the church not only empowered to spread the Good News, but also to once again find unity, to recover, and revitalize its zeal, not because it is needed now but because it is clearly God's intended purpose for the Church since the beginning, for all times.

Rich's style is often didactic, hammering home key points and expanding and building on them as the theme develops. There are some detailed prescriptions for applying the gifts in a contemporary context. Yet there is more in his style that needs to be understood. He naturally writes in the long-standing tradition of the Christian divines and mystics. He skillfully combines his knowledge of Scripture coupled with decades of experience of ministry in the Church with his own testimony of encountering God in his personal journey. One finds in his work remarkable similarity to teachers of antiquity in an almost surprising manner, considering that Pastor Rich speaks from an experience within part of Christ's Church that is not well known for embracing older ecclesiastical approaches to Scripture. But this is merely a confirmation of his willingness to submit and test all things according to Scripture, the common root, source, and rule of all Christian teaching. This common source has led Rich to a common

Prologue

ground where Christians of many backgrounds can meet him. Thus, it would be a mistake to say that this work is only directed toward those within the Charismatic or post-Charismatic movement. Rather, there are points presented here that have relevance to any Christian seeking teaching on the gifts and more particularly the prophetic gift.

As Pastor Rich's oldest son, I can testify to the remarkable grace that God has in His sovereignty allowed my Father to enjoy over many years and am well pleased to read Rich's own witness of that grace. I feel that this work is long overdue.

This book serves as a reminder that God requires holiness and intimacy for His Kingdom and that His equipping ministries will be unfaithful to His call and unsuccessful in changing the world without them.

In His service,
Rev. Troy Harris
Melbourne, Australia

Introduction

What is a paradigm shift of prophetic revelation? To ensure that we are all on the same page in understanding the prophetic, let me take a few moments and establish some foundational concepts of this book. Prophecy or prophetic ministry is a gift of the Holy Spirit mentioned by Paul the apostle in 1 Corinthians 12. Anyone filled with the Holy Spirit can prophesy. Prophecy is God speaking His heart, mind, and purposes to man to reveal Himself to the Church and the world. Such speaking is what the Holy Spirit of God reveals to the one prophesying to others the will of God to build them up, encourage, or release peace and well-being into their lives (see 1 Corinthians 12:10; 14:1-3). Another aspect of prophecy today is a calling to function as a prophet in a governmental capacity that sees, hears, and is inspired by the Holy Spirit to equip the Body of Christ in knowing the voice of God for themselves in their daily lives (see 1 Corinthians 12:28; Ephesians 4:11-16). Those of us involved in the prophetic renewal of the 1970's to 1990's experienced many shifts, changes, and directions in prophetic ministry. Such changes were the need for equipping those called to prophetic ministry, building the character and nature of Jesus in those who prophesy, and pointing them to the Kingdom purposes of the New Covenant in lieu of the Old Covenant. Included in the changes was reading and studying the prophetic Scriptures in the Bible we discovered different types of prophetic speaking, acts, and demonstrations of God's voice and power. We found some prophets to be inspired speakers, other who were called seers of dreams, visions, trances, and some who demonstrated through their mysterious acts or lifestyles a statement of God's heart for Israel and other peoples. In the Old Covenant we

A Paradigm Shift of Prophetic Revelation

see mysterious acts such as God commanding Ezekiel to shave his hair and beard, then weigh and burn part of it representing God's righteous judgments of Israel's rebellions (see Ezekiel 5:1-8). In the New Covenant we find Agabus picking up Paul's belt and binding his own hands and feet representing the Jews binding Paul in Jerusalem (see Acts 21:10-11).

Because of these mysterious acts and declarations associated with prophetic ministry, not all believers and followers of Christ understand the term "prophetic," which is simply hearing, knowing, and understanding the Lord's voice and the various ways He speaks to us so that we can speak or demonstrate His intent to His Church.

A paradigm shift in prophetic revelation can be defined as a fundamental change in the approach to or underlying assumptions of something. In the prophetic renewal, we have seen changes in the pattern, example, or model explained in the above paragraph. Something that we can follow such as model or pattern that gives us a specific direction or plan to follow. In the prophetic realm, everyone who is called to prophetic ministry develop a model or pattern by the way God speaks to them and through them. This is called revelation, as it reveals something from God to the minister through a specific way God communicates to that prophet. Prophetic revelation can come in the form of seeing or hearing. For example, the prophet Amos was called a seer (Hebrew - *chozeh*) or one who receives a communication from God that comes through a visual component that may include a dream, a vision, or a trance (see Numbers 12:6). Not all prophets are seers, but all seers are prophets. Another way God speaks to a prophet (Hebrew - *Nabi*) is through inspiration by the Spirit giving them the verbal component of divine utterance of God's will, intent, and purpose to the hearer. These are two very common ways that God speaks to the prophetic minister, thus they are typical paradigms of prophetic revelation.

The purpose of this book is to examine, study, and bring into practical use and understanding the various ways in which God speaks to the believer today. There are different kinds of visions

Introduction

or dreams and ways of inspired speaking that are discussed and explained that most followers of Christ have not been taught. One of the goals of this book is to clarify these paradigms so that the Body of Christ can function in her full capacity. It is necessary for the believing Church to know that God not only speaks to us through the written word (the Bible) but has in these days released other ways to hear Him. Acts 2:16-21 states,

> *And it shall come to pass in the last days, says God, that I will pour out of My Spirit on all flesh; Your sons and your daughters shall prophesy, your young men shall see visions, your old men will dream dreams, and on My men servants and on My maidservants I will pour out My Spirit in those days; I will show wonders in heaven above and signs in the earth beneath: blood and fire and vapor of smoke. The sun shall be turned into darkness, and the moon into blood, before the coming of the great and awesome day of the Lord and it shall come to pass that whoever calls on the name of the Lord shall be saved.*

These manifest ways of God speaking to the church will be used to glorify and understand the ways of God in the New Covenant Church. Through this current outpouring of His Spirit, the prophetic voice and acts of the church will reveal the nature and power of God above all false gods, thus bringing those who will call upon the name of the Lord to be saved.

Rich Harris

A Paradigm Shift of Prophetic Revelation

Chapter 1

First Steps in a New Nature

I have been crucified with Christ; it is no longer I who live, but Christ lives in me; and the life which I now live in the flesh I live by faith in the Son of God, who loved me and gave Himself for me (Galatians 2:20).

Becoming Childlike

I remember teaching our children to take their first steps as they discovered the thought of mobility and learning how to walk. The experience of assisting their first wobbles across the room is challenging for both parent and child alike. Walk a few steps, fall, move to a crawl, then get up and take a few more steps. Over and over, they proudly learned the disciplines of growing in their infant stages of life. There were always many falls before they became confident that they could walk without the assistance of their parents. Similarly, many repetitive and loving disciplines occurred when teaching them their first words and helping them develop a good vocabulary. As their lives progressed, they were challenged with various falls and mistakes in growing toward their adulthood. The early years with our children were most fruitful as we bonded with them in a loving relationship while helping them learn and grow.

Our first spiritual steps can be awkward as well, especially when we are on an unknown path. Without the aid of an experienced guide on that path, we can easily get off course and find ourselves on

A Paradigm Shift of Prophetic Revelation

unstable ground. Jesus, in reference to our own relationship in His Kingdom here on earth, encouraged us to be childlike:

> ³Truly I say to you, unless you are converted and become like children, you will not enter the kingdom of heaven. ⁴Whoever then humbles himself as this child, he is the greatest in the kingdom of heaven (Matthew 18:3-4).

The nature of a child is pure and unassuming because they have no agenda but to be loved and nurtured, so having an experienced guide is especially important for a child learning to take his first steps. Children need true parental love so that they can respond to that love in return. When genuine love is received, genuine love is always returned because that is the way we are created. Children are born innocent, so they need mature relational nurturing, guidance, and instruction for life and enduring love. Parental love given in the form of gentleness, kindness, patience, meekness, and self-control enables children to bear the best fruit as they grow into adulthood. Real parental love comes from the very heart of our loving Father God.

The process of maturing in life takes many years. There comes a time when parents release their children into the world with confidence that they have done their part in helping them develop so that they can govern themselves. Although children have made the leap to being on their own, parents remain steadfast and are always ready to encourage and support them as they encounter the stumbling blocks of life. True maturity is a long process; it happens when every step is followed by another.

The Christian life is very much the same. We begin as babes in Christ and through years of relational life with God, we learn about the Father's true nature and develop into mature believers. There are first steps in every new level of spiritual growth as a Christian, and we have a Father and a Brother who is also our Savior and Friend to show us the way. We also have a Helper on the journey to

Chapter 1 - First Steps in a New Nature

teach us and give us guidance and wisdom from the Godhead. This relationship with the Trinity is greater than any human relationship and one that should encourage the world toward godly relationships. True believers who demonstrate this Christian lifestyle should be the strongest, most loving and encouraging people in the world. Unfortunately, some Christians today are robbed of the process of spiritual growth and are, therefore, stymied in their true identity in Christ. Regrettably, they remain in the primary stages of the Christian lifestyle defined above.

The Promise of Maturity and Transformation

For myself and many others, moving toward spiritual maturity is an ongoing journey in understanding and living in the mystical nature of Jesus. His loving heart is so complex that every time I think I come near maturity, I find myself lacking in another area of His divine nature. As I reflect back, I realize that my primary discipleship began before I was a true follower of Christ. I was seeing and experiencing His kindness and love in those who carried a part of His divine nature. Even when I was very young, my grandmother and other believing family members were molding me toward my future life in Him. I was being discipled through their words and their Christ-like nature.

Interestingly, the 12 men Jesus called to walk closely with Him were discipled in the same way. They lived their daily lives with Him before the redemptive work of the Cross took place. The disciples learned by listening, watching, and doing what Jesus gave them authority to do. Amazingly, before His death, burial, and resurrection, only two of them realized that He was their promised Messiah. For them, just being in His presence and living life on a daily basis with Him was the beginning of their experiencing His unique characteristics. They learned of Him through relational experience and His demonstrating to them how to live life in the likeness of Kingdom sonship. Jesus' declaration to them was *"Most*

A Paradigm Shift of Prophetic Revelation

assuredly, I say to you, he who believes in Me, the works that I do he will do also, and greater works than these he will do, because I go to My Father" (John 14:12). This was not a leisurely statement made at a Christian conference. The entire promise was based on their living relationship with the Anointed One of God. He was God in the flesh passing the baton of Kingdom power and authority to those who believed in Him through a living relationship with Him. This is the root of the Christian life in the believer.

The goal of every believer in Christ is to emulate a lifestyle of the character and likeness of the Messiah Jesus. We become anointed ones through the transformation of our hearts and minds as we abide in the Anointed One of God. Abiding is a key to our relationship with Christ for it means that we literally become a dwelling place for His life, nature, and power. To remain in His life as our permanent dwelling place is a conscious choice. What we often misunderstand is that this dwelling (abiding) position is more than a mental acknowledgment but is an absolute promise regarding our new life in a Kingdom that cannot be shaken. It is written and decreed that everyone who believes and abides in Him is given grace to share life in the divine nature of God in an unshakable Kingdom (see Hebrews 12:27-29; 2 Peter 1:1-10.) This is part of the first steps of maturing from a prophetic gifting into a prophetic lifestyle. 2 Peter 1:1-4 states:

> *To those who have obtained like precious faith with us by the righteousness of our God and Savior Jesus Christ: Grace and peace be multiplied to you in the knowledge of God and Jesus our Lord, as His divine power has given us all things that pertain to life and godliness, through the knowledge of Him who called us by glory and virtue, by which have been given to us exceedingly great and precious promises that through these you may be partakers of the divine nature having escaped the corruption of the world through lust.*

Chapter 1 - First Steps in a New Nature

One of these precious promises is that of abiding in Him. When we choose to remain in the habitat of the divine nature of God, we are daily changed into His image and likeness. Paul states: *"Therefore we do not lose heart. Even though our outward man is perishing, yet the inward man is being renewed day by day"* (2 Corinthians 4:16). This is simply another precious promise of the benefit of abiding in Him and allowing Him to remain in us. When this promise becomes life to us, in us, and through us, there will be no reason to lose heart.

The apostle Paul writes more encouraging words to us through his writings to the church at Colossae about our relationship with Jesus: *"For in Him dwells all the fullness of the Godhead bodily; and you are complete in Him, who is the head of all principality and power"* (Colossians 2:9-10). Being complete in Christ is the key and the means to being filled to the fullest. God desires to fill us with His nature, love, likeness, and kindness.

John, the apostle of love, writes another truth about our dwelling in the Beloved Christ: *"Love has been perfected among us in this: that we may have boldness in the day of judgment; because as He is, so are we in this world"* (1 John 4:17). This is a present-future word to us because as we live in His likeness and nature here on earth, we will have boldness in the coming day of judgment. Because of our continual spiritual growth in this time, boldness and assurance of His likeness will be manifest to us on the day of judgment.

What magnificent promises of our calling to His glorious nature! Much of today's church is taught that we cannot live in His likeness and nature in this lifetime. I cannot remember how many times I have heard those negative words spoken from the pulpit or from someone in a leadership position. My reaction as a young believer was always, "Then why are you teaching us that if something is in the Bible, it is true?" I, like many others, became frustrated with such controversy concerning the nature of God that the Bible stated as our inherited destiny of becoming like Him. Deep in my heart of hearts, I believed that I was most certainly called to become like Him. Years passed in this battle for my true identity as a believer and friend of

Jesus Christ. As I write this, I am 70 years young and truly see His life forming in my daily thoughts and actions. While on this journey I did determine that the Bible is true and I can abide in Him and experience His presence every day. Even in life's trials, I can abide in Him for He promised He would never leave me or forsake me.

Moving Into His Nature

> *Therefore, **if anyone is in Christ he is a new creation;** old things have passed away; behold all things have become new (2 Corinthians 5:17, emphasis added).*

Our first steps in developing the prophetic gift are to accept the new creation process, which is the development of Christ's nature in our lives. I am not talking about head knowledge of His nature; I am referring to a lifestyle of His likeness in our everyday activity. Second Corinthians 5:17 is a present-future word: we are in Christ now, and we are becoming a new creation day by day. However, as sons and daughters of God, there is a part of having our minds renewed to the thoughts and intentions of the Father's heart. Our relationship with Christ is essential to becoming like Him. His disciples followed Him for 3 1/2 years. During that time, He taught them the ways and nature of God through the demonstration of His life in the Father (see John 14:10-12). We must consider that the 3 1/2 years were not enough time for them to come to the fullness of Christ. Further things were necessary as He gave promise of the Helper, the Holy Spirit, whom the Father would send in His name (see John 14:25-26.) The Holy Spirit must become our Teacher, Counselor, and Friend as John 16:13-15 emphasizes:

> *However, when He, the Spirit of truth, has come, He will guide you into all truth; for He will not speak on His own authority, but whatever He hears He will speak; and He*

Chapter 1 - First Steps in a New Nature

will tell you things to come. He will glorify Me, for He will take of what is Mine and declare it to you. All things that the Father has are Mine. Therefore I said that He will take of Mine and declare it to you.

For more than half my life as a believer, this has been a personal standard for me. This portion of Scripture has aided me in understanding the various ways in which God can speak to us. It also has helped me to know and understand the nature of the Holy Spirit in relationship to the Father and the Son.

When we look at the work of the Holy Spirit concerning our life in Christ, John 16:13-15 must become a standard for guiding us into all truth. First, He leads us to the truth about our lives not as sinners but as those redeemed by Christ. In verse 13, Jesus speaks that the Holy Spirit is the Spirit of Truth, and He only leads us into the truth. It is not His nature to lead us to anything but the truth of who Christ is and who we are becoming through abiding in Him. It is astonishing to me that the Holy Spirit does not speak to us on His Own accord but precisely says the things He hears from the Father and the Son. Knowing this and practicing this truth helps build confidence in our ongoing relationship with God the Father, God the Son and God the Holy Spirit. As we continue to commune daily with the Spirit of God, He promises to show us things to come. Not just future prophetic events, but things concerning our own life, thus helping us to progress into the nature and likeness of Jesus. These godly thoughts and spiritual manifestations come to us in the various ways the Spirit speaks to us such as the still small voice, dreams, visions and divine appointments. We will cover these spiritual activities more specifically in another part of this book.

Next, the Holy Spirit receives everything from the Godhead that pertains to life and godliness in Christ and makes them known to us. His position in the Godhead is the voice who speaks for Jesus: *"He will take of what is Mine (everything belonging to the whole nature of Jesus) and* **declare it to you"** (John 16:14, author's paraphrase).

A Paradigm Shift of Prophetic Revelation

What a majestic show of God's desire and intent to have an open and transparent relationship with us. For God to declare to us the very nature, likeness, thoughts, and power of His Son via the Holy Spirit is in itself a miraculous work. It is extraordinary that some in the Body of Christ cannot comprehend God giving such a promise. When we begin to see and accept this act of divine intervention as being God's relational kindness toward us as His children, we are changed. Our hearts and minds are transformed into the image of Jesus' nature on earth as it is in heaven—in us. This is the Father's great desire for us, and the Holy Spirit is His active agent who brings heaven to earth in divine intervention. God speaks to our spirit through His indwelling Spirit renewing our mind to His Own thoughts and intents.

We must consider in this Scripture that everything we hear from the Holy Spirit will always glorify Jesus. Knowing and practicing this helps us know the voice of God in our personal lives and prophecy. The Holy Spirit can do nothing to dishonor Jesus or the Father because His Own nature is in the life of the Godhead. Any time we hear, sense, or see (spiritually) something that would dishonor the Godhead, it will not be from the Holy Spirit. This is why Jesus said of Him that He (the Holy Spirit) has all the life in the Father and the Son as His Own (see John 16:14-15). It is from the divine position of God's Own nature that the Holy Spirit declares and shows to us what is in the mind and heart of the Godhead. When a prophetic person knows Father's intent about a person, group, or situation, our words will bring change.

Understanding the Father's purpose requires walking in a relationship with Him. Our relationship must mirror that which He had with Jesus as the Son of Man. He is more than willing to share His heart, mind, and intentions with us. We have barely scratched the surface of God's love toward us. We can see it when we learn to rest and find our peace in the quietness of our relationship with the Godhead. The Holy Spirit holds the key to the mysteries of God for which we all desire to know and to see. *"But God has revealed them to us through His Spirit. For the Spirit searches all things, (hidden in*

Chapter 1 - First Steps in a New Nature

the depth of God's being) yes the deep things of God" (1 Corinthians 1:10, emphasis added). How deep in Him are we prepared or willing to go?

Finally, in verse 15, Jesus seals the power and authority given to us in our relationship with the Holy Spirit. Jesus alludes to His intimate position in the Godhead by saying that the Father hides nothing from the Son except that which is otherwise declared in Scripture. Whatever the Father reveals to the Son (see John 5:19; 6:38; 7:16; 8:28), the Holy Spirit has authority to reveal to us whenever the Godhead chooses to do so. At this prompting of His voice, we hear and do just as Jesus heard and did. There are no limits to what God desires to reveal to His prophetic sons and daughters. However, experience tells us that He will not give us something to handle with godly character and integrity beyond our maturity in Christ. We know that the Holy Spirit always glorifies Jesus, so we should do the same. This is our identity as sons of the living God, YHVH (sometimes translated Jehovah). As we live our lives in Christ, the indwelling Spirit will live God's life in us, to us, and through us.

Identity Theft

In today's world, there is great concern about identity theft. Having our identities stolen consists of losing our finances, important and personal information, and details about our lives. Through taking our identity, the thief takes on our life information and makes it their own causing to lose our bank accounts, using our personal information to create lines of credit to purchase expensive items for their own use under the victim's name. Unfortunately, the church is subject to having our true identities stolen through deception, false teaching, denominations, and adopting worldly mindsets. Worldly mindsets create an emphasis on such things as living the American dream of having everything we want. Without the wisdom of God the American dream creates a focus on the things of the world rather than the Kingdom of God (see Matthew 6:25-34). Jesus made it clear that Satan the thief comes to steal, kill, and destroy (see John 10:10). When our true identity is stolen, we lose the power and authority that comes from our knowing who He is in and through us. Jesus said, *"All power and authority has been given to Me in heaven and earth"* (Matthew 28:18). He then commands his disciples to go into the world with His authority and do the things He did while being God in the flesh here on earth. If our identity as believers is in anything other than Him and the authority He gives us, we have no power to overcome the Satan, the god of this world.

Through many years of equipping and mentoring prophetic people, I realized there was a lie that was misleading us in the development of prophecy—identity theft had crept into the church. The thief had stolen our true identity and replaced it with the diversion of good and proper titles. Some students who come to our ministry school have an excitement of being involved in prophecy and have their ideas about what it means to be a prophet. They are more interested in their identity being the gift than in the character to adequately support the gift. They want the identity and recognition of a prophet without the nature of Jesus. Experience has taught me that there is often a wrong mindset about the identity of prophets in the church.

Many believers today base their identities on their professional or occupational titles, spiritual gifts, or callings. Similar to a worldly position like an architect, we tend to make that title an emphasis of who we are rather than it being our profession or occupation. The same takes place in the church when our gift becomes our identity rather than it simply being one function of Christ in us. I have found that one can be very gifted in prophecy but lack the character and nature of Jesus in their lives.

Overemphasizing identity in one's gift can overwhelm the church and draw people to the gift and title of the individual. Many ministers and ministries today are given exaggerated promotion or publicity, which, in turn, causes the church to look at the ministries rather than at Christ who they should truly represent. The minister,

Chapter 1 - First Steps in a New Nature

then, becomes the focus of many in the church in lieu of Christ who is the new life of all true ministers. God's purpose of the born again experience is to change us into the image, life, and likeness of Christ. In that encounter with God we become manifest sons of God. The mystery of this exchanged life in Christ becomes our real identity with a lesser emphasis on our particular function in ministry. Christ is our living example of the true ministry of God in the flesh. We become like Him!

Our emphasis on the title rather than the character and nature of Christ has caused problems in the prophetic movement today. We must address this because the words that flow from our mouths are mixed with the condition of our heart (see Matthew 12:33-37). True prophetic words come from the heart of God to our spirit, but if our character lacks that of Jesus' nature, the prophecy is often infected with our present character. The character of a prophetic person must exceed our love for the gift given to us.

Our identity comes from being rooted and grounded in Christ (see Ephesians 4:11-13). Our goal is to be a mature follower of Christ. We must work toward the goal of finding the key to our individual lives—rooted and grounded in the Lord's kindness, mercy, compassion, love, and character. Doing this requires a commitment to an intimate relationship with Him on a daily basis. We must not be committed to Him religiously, but relationally. I would like to say it is day by day, but more realistically it is moment by moment.

In moves of God over the past few centuries, man has adopted a false identity in our relationship with God based on the theme of that move rather than our identity in Christ. The prophetic movement of our time has done much of the same in that suddenly everything has become prophetically oriented. Once again, this mindset affects our true identity in Christ. The apostle Paul recognized this problem in the churches he helped establish. He gave a teaching on this theme to the church at Rome and Ephesus. To Rome, he wrote *"And do not be conformed to the ways of this world, but be transformed by the renewing of your mind, that you may prove what is that good and*

A Paradigm Shift of Prophetic Revelation

acceptable and perfect will of God" (Romans 12:2). In his letter to the Ephesians, he said, *"Put off, concerning your former conduct, the old man which grows corrupt according to the deceitful lusts, and be renewed in the spirit of your mind"* (Ephesians 4:22-23). The point from both of these references is that we cannot sway from God's purpose for our identity by conforming to a movement or event of God. When we are focused on a living relationship with Jesus and understanding His nature, we are on the path to having our mind renewed to the way He lives and thinks. Knowing and living this is vital for the prophet and the prophetic student.

As mentioned earlier, many believers in Christ have established their identity based on their denomination, title, position, career, spiritual gift, or calling. Our conversion experience is simply this: *"I have died (to the old Adamic nature), and my life is hidden with Christ in God"* (Colossians 3:3, author's paraphrase). Understanding the essence of our new life and identity is to know the reality that *"I have been crucified with Christ; it is no longer I who live, but Christ lives in me; and the life which I now live in the flesh I live by faith in the Son of God who loved me and gave Himself for me"* (Galatians 2:20). Paul understood that his identity was not in being an apostle of Christ but that the very life of Christ was being lived in and through him. Who he was in the past was no longer a consideration in his new life in Christ. He was not only being conformed to the image of Christ's life, but was first being conformed to the image of His death. Philippians 3:10 states, *"that I may know Him and the power of His resurrection, and the fellowship of His suffering, being conformed to the image of His death."* Paul understood that his old Pharisaical lifestyle had been put in the grave and could not be a part of the new man God had called him to be. Until we understand our true identity through His death and begin to live our lives in His life, our identity will be in meaningless titles and positions.

Identity theft is a major pitfall in the Body of Christ, resulting in our losing godly power and authority in the earth today. If our identity is in anything other than Christ and the power of His resurrection, we can only minister to others in our power. For instance, if my identity is in my denomination, I will only be able to minister in the beliefs of that faith. Wrong identities limit the truth and power of Christ in us. However, if our identity is that we now have His life in us, then there is no limit to what He can do through us as vessels of His life and presence.

We are not to take on the image of a movement or a gift; we are to be conformed to the image and likeness of Christ. Christ-likeness should be an emphasis in prophetic ministry because it brings maturity and purity that is a vital part of advancing the Kingdom of God. Christ is the identity and character we seek to portray through a life lived in the Father's love, character and wisdom in each of our relationships (see John 14:9; Hebrews 1:2-3). When those in prophetic ministry abide in Him as their true identity and nature, prophecy will take a giant step toward the full intent of God to be His spokesperson.

Disciplines of Practice

For us to walk in the nature of Christ, there must be areas of spiritual disciplines in our life. Prayer is a discipline and commitment and it leads to a closer relationship with God. Prayer is communication with God that we can enjoy daily and it plays a vital role in our relationship with the Father. Our identity in Christ is our identity in prayer. Because all believers take on the likeness of Christ, the Father sees us as sons. In that position, we pray to the Father as sons presenting all that Jesus is as the Son. *"And in that day you will ask Me nothing. Most assuredly, I say to you,* **whatever you ask the Father in My name** *He will give you. Until now you have asked nothing in My name. Ask, and you will receive, that your joy may be full"* (John 16:23-24).

When I was a young believer in Christ, I learned something imperative about prayer. Prayer, no matter what type (petition, declaration, intercession), is always a dialogue with God, not a monologue with our thoughts and desires. Prayer is simply having a conversation with God and conversations involve both speaking and listening. Most of us know how to speak well in prayer but lack in the discipline of listening. Our busy lifestyle in the West is one of constant noise that interrupts the art of listening and our prayer life suffers much by not hearing God's voice. It is our responsibility to choose to make time to commune in beautiful dialogue with our wonderful Father.

I have a pastor friend who oversees a large church in South-Central Colorado. This church has three Sunday services and another on Saturday night. He ministers at each of these services plus has certain pastoral responsibilities during the week such as overseeing a large administrative and pastoral staff. I admire this man because I know that he often takes personal time away from the busyness of church responsibilities and goes to a quiet, rustic camp in the nearby mountains where he spends several days calming his soul and resting in the presence of the Lord. When he returns to his ministry responsibilities, he is refreshed in spirit, soul, and body. His prayer life is a demonstration of living a Christ-like lifestyle. I believe this is a key for the health and growth of the church he oversees.

If we as prophetic people will commit ourselves to an exact time of dialogue with God, we will hear Him more clearly for ourselves and others. Jesus is the model of the New Covenant prophet and He had an ongoing dialogue with the Father. In that dialogue we can assume that He spoke to the Father about such things as: "What would You have Me do in this situation with these religious Pharisees?" "Show Me who You desire to touch today and how You want to heal them." As He waits and listens He might have heard this: "Today You will meet a blind man on the way to the fish market. You must first proclaim that 'As long as I Am in the world, I Am the light of the world.' Then I want You to spit on the ground and make mud packs from Your saliva, place them on his eyes and direct him to wash in the pool of Siloam. When the man does this, he will receive his healing. Son, remember I Am the light of the world and I AM

Chapter 1 - First Steps in a New Nature

in You. This is a point of healing the blind so that they may see the light."

Jesus' entire ministry was based on what He heard, saw, and was taught by the Father during His time of dialoguing with Him. As we look at His life, we see that He would often go off by Himself to pray. Unlike many today who say things like, "I will have to pray about that," Jesus dialogued with the Father simply because they are One, and we are one with Them through the finished work of the Cross. Thus, we also can have an ongoing dialogue with the Father as we walk through the menial tasks of our daily lives (see John 17:20-23). We should continue to take the time to go off to our place of silence from the world. Jesus' lifestyle of continuous dialogue with the Father takes discipline and an intimate relationship and is vital for us to learn and practice.

As a prophetic person, I have daily dialogues with the Father. If I plan to go hiking today, I don't have to pray or talk to Him about whether or not to put on hiking shoes if I am going on an unpaved trail. However, I may not know about a possible divine appointment while on that trail. To know what my Father's intent is for me on that day, I might inquire: "Father what is Your purpose for my life today?" Wait and listen for the answer and then perhaps pray, "Father, on my hike today I ask for a divine appointment that would glorify You and Your Son. I so love You!" When I get to the end of that trail, I will rest in Him and whatever works He did through my obedience to His voice that day. When I rest in His Word and His work I am proclaiming the life of one, *"who is more than a conqueror through Him who loves me"* (Romans 8:37).

Prayer, regardless of the type, is simply dialoguing with the Father. In doing this, I am proclaiming my Kingdom sonship as Jesus taught us: *"And in that day you will ask Me nothing. Most assuredly, I say to you, whatever you ask the Father in My name He will give you. Until now you have asked nothing in My name. Ask, and you will receive, that your joy may be full"* (John 16:23-24). Sonship is what the whole creation longs to experience (see Romans 8:18-22).

A Paradigm Shift of Prophetic Revelation

Humility

Humility, the absolute absence of self-assurance, is a much needed characteristic for prophetic ministry. It is essential to our maturity as a prophetic minister.

Moses and Jesus truly lived in godly humility. Jesus, although He was God, took upon Himself the body of human flesh and made Himself of *no reputation* and came to us as a bondservant (see Philippians 2:6-7). Moses wrote that he, himself, was a humble man. Perhaps that is why God chose him to lead His people through the wilderness to the Land of Promise (see Numbers 12:3). The Hebrew word for Moses' humility is *kana,* meaning to be humbled and subdued in nature. Humility is the absence of self-assurance and self-righteousness and is necessary for purity in a prophetic lifestyle. Just as the human body does not rely only on individual muscles for its absolute strength, but on all its vital parts, so must we rely on Father and the other members of the Body for our wholeness. Humility is not something we can muster up on our own, especially in prophetic ministry and hearing God's voice. We cannot study a book on how to become a prophet and then prophesy without the intervention of God's Spirit. Hearing God's voice in any form involves a relationship with the Godhead through the indwelling Holy Spirit. God speaks through His prophets by His Spirit in them (see Nehemiah 9:30). In the Old Covenant, God's Spirit entered into the prophets, and they spoke by the unction of the Spirit entering them or coming upon them. Today, God's Spirit dwells in us, and we can all hear His voice because we have a better Covenant with better promises.

Growing in the Word

The Living Word is Jesus, for it is written, *"That which was from the beginning, which we have heard, which we have seen with our eyes, which we have looked upon, and our hands have handled, concerning the Word of Life"* (1 John 1:1). The written word (Greek *logos*-Hebrew *dabar*) is the Living Word as written in the Bible. In the New Covenant writings, it is evident that the ultimate revelation of "the Word of God" is fulfilled in Jesus Christ, the incarnation of the divine Word. Jesus is also the *rhema* (a Greek word denoting that which is uttered in speech or writing) as expressed in the spoken words of Jesus in the context of His public speaking and preaching ministry. *Rhema* also refers to words spoken in the context of apostolic preaching.

The Living Word, Jesus, must be the primary expression of the prophetic words that come out of our mouths. For Jesus said, *"It is the Spirit who gives life; the flesh profits nothing. The words that I speak are spirit, and they are life"* (John 6:63). The prophetic words we speak must also bring Spirit and life to the hearer. We are prophetic representatives in Christ expressing the thoughts, purposes, and intents of God through the operation of the Spirit in prophetic utterance. Remember, the flesh profits nothing and if we mix our thoughts with God's thoughts, then the word is diluted from the purity in which God originally intended.

In the written Word lives the very life and thoughts of God. It is vital that we consume the Word as a daily diet because it has the power to transform our minds. The apostle Paul wrote that in the process of that transformation, our minds are renewed to prove what is the good and acceptable and perfect (mature) will of God. If we do not know the Word of God, how can we speak for the God of the Word? Over a period of 25 years or more, I have observed many prophetically gifted people speak in such a way that their lack of knowledge and wisdom of God's Word is clearly evident. Why is this? I believe it is because they refuse to go through the process of developing their prophetic gift. They see it as their gift and take personal possession of it for their benefit. We live in a culture where the process of maturing requires too much work, time, and effort. Recently, I had a conversation with a young man who had just graduated from a Bible college. He wasn't sure what his ministry or calling was, and so I asked him what his major had been in school. He said it was youth ministry. After I suggested to him that there was still a process to go through to be seasoned in his chosen field, he said, "my generation does not like or want the process." What he got in his Christian college was a theory with little practical application in the study of God's Word. We must realize why it is so important to us not just to know ideas of God's Word but study and meditate on it as we grow in our prophetic gifting.

Our first steps toward developing our prophetic gifting are being rooted in the foundations of our lifestyle with and in Christ and His love, character, nature, and likeness. We must be willing to allow Him, through the exchanged life (ours for His), to form us into the divine nature promised to the believer. That is:

> *Grace and peace be multiplied to you in the knowledge of God and of Jesus our Lord, as His divine power has given us all things that pertain to life and godliness, through the knowledge of Him who called us by glory and virtue, by which have been given to us exceedingly great and precious promises, that through these you may be partakers of the divine nature, having escaped the corruption that is in the world through lust (2 Peter 1:2-4).*

These words of God's promises toward us are essential for our development in the prophetic arena.

Prayer

Father, help us to take one step at a time in our spiritual journey toward living in the nature of Your beloved Son, Jesus. We thank You for the work and purpose of the Holy Spirit leading us to the thoughts, intents, and purposes of sons and daughters who are being conformed daily, even moment by moment, into the likeness and image of our beloved Friend and Savior, Jesus Christ.

Father, we love You and our desire is toward You and Your intent that our lives be complete in the fullness of the Godhead bodily as Your

Scriptures teach us. Thank You for speaking to us via the Holy Spirit, dreams, visions, and the many ways You show Your life to us as Your prophetic people. Let our words be only the intent of Your heart and truly reflect Your love.

    Amen

Chapter 2

Comprehending Prophecy

Worship God! For the testimony of Jesus is the spirit of prophecy. (Revelation 19:10b).

The subject and practice of prophecy remains an enigma for much of today's Church. While in the last 30 years (from the 1980's to the present) significant progress has been made in developing God's prophetically gifted people. During this process, a handful of faithful ministries obeyed the commissioned call to equip us in this vital spiritual gift and ministry. Currently, I believe we have only scratched the surface of our Father's desire for the Kingdom purpose of prophecy.

The Lord is intentional with us about prophetic development continuing in the Church. He desires to see those endowed with prophecy to come to maturity in Christ's character and our prophetic gift. This is clearly stated for us in Ephesians 4:13, *"until we all arrive at the unity implied by trusting and knowing the Son of God, at full manhood, at the standard of maturity set by the Messiah's perfection"* (CJB). I love this translation as it makes clear the intent of God pointing toward our fully knowing Jesus, the fullness of godly manhood set by the standard of His perfection (fully man, fully God). That is the intent and goal of the Godhead to which we are brought into godly, Christ-like maturity. This includes the development of prophetic ministry. Scripture and experience clearly show us the pathway of ministering prophetically is not an easy one. And in that sometimes narrow path, God is not just developing our gift but is intentionally challenging our lives to build in us the character of His beloved Son. For some who are endowed with this gift, the road is long, enduring the entirety of their spiritual life in Christ. For others, it may be for a short season, a specific time, place, or people group. From Moses to Jesus and with current-day prophetic ministers, prophecy is still misunderstood by many Christians and church leaders.

There is no doubt that God, through His redemption and love, has created the time, place, and ministers to equip us in the process of developing prophecy. His intent is clearly written in the Scriptures beginning with the teaching of Moses. We read in Numbers 11:29 where, after a controversy among the people concerning God's direction and purpose for their lives and in answer to Moses' desire, God puts the Spirit of prophecy upon the 70 elders. These elders assisted Moses for the time in prophetically speaking specific issues of God's intent for the people. Suddenly, Moses proclaims the very heart of God for all of Israel. *"Are you zealous for my sake? Oh, that all the Lord's people were prophets and that the Lord would put His Spirit upon them!"* Moses knew that prophecy was the power to release God's spoken will for any given situation in Israel's wilderness journey.

Notice here in the Old Covenant that God put or set His Spirit upon them. This is significantly different than the pouring out of His Spirit upon the New Covenant Church. In the Old Covenant, He set His Spirit upon those called to prophesy at His will because of the people's need to hear Him with the objective to return them to right relationship with Him. Clearly in that Covenant, God spoke to His prophets Spirit to spirit: *"Yet for many years You had patience with them,* **(the Hebrew people)***, and testified against them by Your Spirit in Your prophets"* (Nehemiah 9:30, emphasis added). The prophets testified against them with the intent to bring them back into covenant with God.

The New Covenant promises greatly exceed that of the Old, yet it was always the heart of God to freely give us of His Spirit. The promise of the Father that Jesus spoke about had to do with blood

Chapter 2 - Comprehending Prophecy

covenant redemption freely causing us to have right relationship with the Godhead. At Pentecost, the Holy Spirit was not just set or put upon us, but was given a dwelling place in us! Spirit to spirit we were transformed into the new nature of Jesus. So, prophecy in this New Covenant has to do with God dwelling in us! Thus, God can speak directly to the spirit of every believer in Christ. So, one may ask, "Why then do we need prophets and prophetic ministry in this Covenant?"

A New Covenant

See Jeremiah 31:31-34; Matthew 26:28. Scripture clearly shows the intent of the Father concerning prophecy in the New Covenant Church. In Ephesians 4:11-13, Paul writes,

> *And He Himself **(Jesus)** gave some to be apostles, **some prophets**, some evangelists, and some pastors and teachers, for the equipping of the saints **(all believers)** for the work of the ministry, for the edifying of the body of Christ, till we all come to the unity of the faith and of the knowledge of the Son of God, to a perfect man, to the measure of the stature of the fullness of Christ (emphasis added).*

These five ministry gifts are functions of the church in God's order and design. They are specific ministries commissioned to equip us in the nature of Christ. Prophets are called to equip the saints in the nature of hearing, knowing, and speaking as God's voice in the Church.

The apostle Paul explains to the church at Corinth that the Holy Spirit is the Person of the Godhead who distributes *the things of the Spirit (gifts)* individually as He wills (1 Corinthians 12:4-11). These *gifts* although resident in the ministry functions mentioned above are unique to and are for every believer. One of those *gifts* is prophecy. Our gracious Father continues to show us His intent for prophecy

A Paradigm Shift of Prophetic Revelation

when Paul writes in 1 Corinthians 14:1 the following: *"Pursue love, and desire spiritual gifts, but especially that you may prophesy."* So we see throughout history God's Kingdom desire for this gift and ministry function. The process of prophetic development and the maturing of prophets remain in our current time and beyond. We will put this in proper perspective in another part of this book. In order to understand prophecy, we must understand God's intent for the gift and its use in the church today.

What we often miss in God's purpose and intent for any area of ministry is the connection and the difference between one Covenant and the other. The Old and the New Covenants are in one book called the Holy Scriptures. Both covenants show us God's heart and intent for a Kingdom people. As a Kingdom emphasis, a new prophetic type was ushered in after John the Baptist (see Luke 16:16). What Jesus said about this significant change was that His Kingdom would now be proclaimed not by one but by many. Clearly at the time of the New Covenant, prophetic ministry remained as the same function—to speak for God—but the message changed. Israel was a type of God's Kingdom prophetically portrayed through the functions of priests and the prophets. They were called to be a kingdom of priests to God. The purpose and function of the priests was:

> *Now therefore if you will indeed obey My **voice** and keep My **covenant** then you shall be a special treasure to Me above all people; for the earth is Mine. And you shall be to Me a kingdom of priests and a holy nation. These are the words which you shall speak to the children of Israel (Exodus 19:5-6 emphasis added).*

The preceding function and call of Israel and that covenant was given to them through Moses the prophet. Moses was God's **voice** giving definition to the **covenant** of God. Moses' statement in Exodus 19:6 was that Israel was to be a people set apart, holy unto God, as representatives of His nature in the earth. God the Father

Chapter 2 - Comprehending Prophecy

set prophets in Israel to be His spokespersons to keep this covenant people as a holy kingdom of priests unto Him. God's intents for the prophetic voices in that Covenant were to turn His people back to the Covenant He made with them.

After John the Baptist, the last of the Old Covenant prophets, the New Covenant was ushered in by Jesus after His childhood and wilderness experiences. His first words were that of a prophetic nature when He said *"Repent for the kingdom of heaven is at hand"* (Matthew 4:17b). In its simplest form, this statement is saying that heaven has come to earth bringing its King who will set up that Kingdom at a later time. Remarkably, the Kingdom of Heaven (or God) came among us (in Christ) and now dwells within us through the work of the Cross and release of the Holy Spirit to dwell in us. Jesus is the model New Covenant prophet setting this covenant in place through His words. If we say that the church today is prophetic in nature, Christ is the reason. *Father God, let Your Kingdom come, let Your will be done on earth, just as it is in heaven right now here today in and among Your church* (author's paraphrase - see Matthew 6:6-15).

The Old Covenant prophets prophesied *about* a coming King and His Kingdom. They also prophesied of repentance toward God through words destined to turn Israel's heart back to His covenant ways. The New Covenant prophets prophesy *in* the King who came and spoke with authority, power, and love. John the Baptist ushered the Kingdom into being and the New Covenant prophets proclaim, declare, and establish God's Kingdom voice here on earth. A primary emphasis of prophecy today is to connect God's people to Him and to His Kingdom. They also equip the Body of Christ in the art of hearing God's voice while turning the church back to the holiness and purity of His intent for the Kingdom. In the infinite wisdom of God, we find the same intent for the prophetically gifted and see an increase and yet a significant change of ministry and purpose in the New Covenant writings. This is simply true because we are living in *"the times of restoration of all things which God has spoken by the mouth of His holy prophets since the world began"* (Acts 3:21b).

A Paradigm Shift of Prophetic Revelation

He is still speaking and demonstrating *"the times of restoration of all things"* through His prophets and believing people today. We are in a position of restoring the Kingdom of God and all things that He is and created life to be in the earth. Restoration does not stop at infancy or youth but sets its goal at maturity in the intentions and works of Christ since the world began.

Called Before Commissioned

My personal call came as a young man in my twenties during the 1960s. At that time, I was involved with a small group of believers meeting in homes and commercial storefront spaces. Over the years, I received dreams and impressions of things that would later occur although I had no real understanding of prophets or the prophetic gift. It was not discussed or considered in the denomination where I was at the time. I had no clue what prophecy meant except that it had a purpose. As I grew spiritually, I began to understand God had a purpose for my life. I also developed a great zeal for God's kind nature of receiving me in His Kingdom as a son! Almost immediately I had great love for Him as a Father, for the Bible, and for prayer; yet something in my church upbringing was missing.

As my zealous search for Him continued, I was suddenly introduced to another baptism. This was of course the baptism of the Holy Spirit and fire that John the Baptist spoke of in the gospels. Along with that and my additional Kingdom perspectives, I began receiving what my mentors of that time termed the *"gifts of the Spirit."* When I received this baptism of the Holy Spirit, almost immediately I began dreaming, having visionary experiences, and seemingly supernatural insight into what appeared to me in my spiritual adolescence as coming from God. This was the beginning of new life for me and yet some of my peers warned me to be careful. But I continued to pursue more of His love and presence in my life. Nearly 30 years later, I was commissioned to His service as a prophetic teacher.

Chapter 2 - Comprehending Prophecy

At the beginning of my learning curve, a prophetic woman involved in the group was my only teacher. In those days, we had no reference to equipping prophetic people. Sometime in 1967, I was given a prophetic word that I would be involved in a school of prophets. There were no specifics as to how that would take place or when. For many years, I wondered when and how this would happen. What in the world would my role be in a school of prophets? Where was this school? In the following years, I began dreaming dreams that seemed to reference the last days. I knew in my spirit I was to be involved with the prophetic, teaching, and healing ministries at a future time.

As this prophetic gift began to develop more in my life, I experienced unusual manifestations of different kinds of spirits. I had received no instruction of dealing with anything unusual in the spiritual realm. Some of these events were frightening and of an evil nature. I was young and inexperienced in what is now termed "spiritual warfare" and the extent of my knowledge at the time was to grab my Bible and cry out the name of Jesus. It worked well in my spiritual adolescence! After several of those experiences, I was awakened one morning around 3 a.m. and saw with my natural eyes a huge angel standing in my room. He was so large that he appeared to go up through the ceiling. As I gazed upon this angelic being, the heavens suddenly seemed to open and I saw what appeared to be the face and shoulders of Jesus. He smiled at me, assuring me that He loved me and that I was safe in His presence. After this visionary appearance, I never again experienced the frightening manifestations. God had assured me that His Son was far above all principalities and powers both in heavenly places and on the earth.

Periodically through the years, I continued to receive dreams, visions, and impressions in the Spirit. Some 20 years later, I began receiving words of knowledge for people and ministries, although most of the time I did not know what to do with them as prophecy was not practiced in most churches I attended. I continued to dream on a regular basis, later realizing most of them were for my own life and future.

The Call of God

There is an intended purpose for the life of every believer, and we know from Scripture that the Holy Spirit gives and distributes spiritual *gifts* as He wills for the benefit of the whole body.

We must remember that the Holy Spirit is a part of the Godhead, and the Father knows us before we are formed in our mother's womb. The life is in the blood, and the blood carries the DNA throughout our bodies. We who believe are destined to the conformity of the spiritual likeness of Christ. Therefore, we must realize that our *gifting* is not our identity but a part of God's intent for us to fulfill our Kingdom purpose. Because God is Spirit, our new DNA comes from Him through the redemptive blood of His beloved Son, Jesus. Realizing this, we know the *gifts* of the Spirit are a part of the very nature, life, and character of God! So along with our call (our destined Kingdom purpose), God gives us by His intent *gifts* of His nature as part of that Kingdom purpose through our redemption. The *gifts* are simply spiritual life tools of Kingdom power that help us live and move in the authority of His Son's Name. Jesus said that those who believe in Him would do the things He did and even greater works (see John 14:12-14). The Holy Spirit is the promise of the Father to endue us with power from on high (see Luke 24:49). In that sovereign act, He also distributes *the things of the Spirit* to empower us in particular characteristics of His nature. Prophecy and the revelatory gifts, along with other *gifts* of the Spirit, are specific characteristics of God. When we refer to revelatory gifts, we are talking about spiritual gifts that reveal the heart, mind, and purposes of God. We will discuss these in detail in Chapter 6 of this book.

It is important for us to realize that our call or gifting come long before our commissioning to God's future Kingdom service or ministry function. For example, Paul was called by God 12 to 14 years before the Lord commissioned him as an apostle. The 12 disciples of Christ had spent at least three and a half years with Him before they were sent out as commissioned apostles. Their commissioning came

Chapter 2 - Comprehending Prophecy

after His resurrection, at the time of the ascension and the release of the indwelling Holy Spirit.

From a New Covenant perspective, we see a time of hands-on equipping done by Jesus. He prepared the 12 for Kingdom service before the empowering of the Holy Spirit. On the day of Pentecost, God released the Holy Spirit and 120 received God's power and commissioning. Commissioning is simply an authorization to certain responsibilities, tasks, or powers. Just like that time, we are given authority in our relationship with Christ and the Godhead to act on behalf of Him who is the authority.

Regarding the Old Covenant, we must understand that those prophets had no indwelling of the Holy Spirit, unlike the New Covenant believer. In the Old Covenant, we find the terms, *"within, on, or upon"* referring to the ministry of a prophet engaged with the Holy Spirit. The Hebrew word is *qereb* meaning, *the inner parts, heart or mind, and often translated as within.* This is from a Hebraic perspective, as this term means *the seat or faculty of thought and emotion.* The Holy Spirit was with them, but did not dwell in them as He does in us who are baptized in Him, thus becoming one with Him.

In Good Company

In the Old Covenant, Samuel is the first mentioned in a training scenario with a company or group of prophets. By God's will to the barren Hannah, Samuel was dedicated to God in his mother's womb. Perhaps this is where we also find that thought as in the life of Jeremiah (see Jeremiah 1:5). However, Samuel grew in the Lord by ministering alongside Eli, the priest. It was in this environment that Samuel learned to approach and respect God's presence; to hear His voice as one who ministered daily to him. Eli trained Samuel to quiet his soul and listen to the Lord's instructions once he recognized God's voice (see 1 Samuel 3:1-19). Samuel's basic training as a forthcoming

A Paradigm Shift of Prophetic Revelation

prophet happened daily working with Eli, the priest. Later Samuel mentored others called to be prophets. He was the first in Scripture to lead a company of prophets.

I want to note here that there is no Hebrew word in the context of Scripture implying a school (place of learning) for prophets. Rather the Hebrew word is *chebel*, literally meaning a rope or something twisted together to be as one strength. Figuratively, *chebel* has the meaning of a company (as if tied together). So, in the cause of having a school of prophets, it is best termed a company or group of prophets. Scripture implies that they were of one kind having the same mind, heart, and purpose. There is great power in this kind of gathering as it changes the atmosphere around us and we begin to sense the presence of God! Samuel was the experienced leader of this group. Because of his training, Samuel intimately knew God's voice, character, and likeness. Intimacy and abiding are key issues in our relationship with the Lord. It is in this kind of bond that we develop relationship in the prophetic realm.

Through my years of experience, training, and active involvement in the prophetic ministry since the 1960s, I have found the Hebraic way of learning the most effective.

The Sons of the Prophets

Elijah, called of God, came out of the wilderness to mentor and train Elisha. We have no record of his training, although Scripture implies a process of calling and teaching in the Old Covenant. Elijah's instruction remains a mystery. At the end of Elijah's term of office and for a peculiar reason, Elisha refers to him as, *"my father, my father."* This statement implies a father/son relationship that was an important part of the Hebrew culture. Fathers instructed their sons about the Scriptures and living a godly life. So, I want to take a moment and investigate the term "sons of the prophets." In Hebrew thought, there are two types of sons. Those born of one's seed and those adopted into one's family. Those named of their father's seed

Chapter 2 - Comprehending Prophecy

are referred to as *a son of* and use the preface of *ben*. Those named as adopted sons of a family are prefaced with *bar* meaning *adopted sons*. Such an example is Jeremiah, son (*ben*) of Hilkiah of the priest (see Jeremiah 1:1).

Further, in the New Covenant, the name Barnabas implies by Hebrew origin an adopted son of a prophet. David Stern's translation (Complete Jewish Bible-CJB) gives us our first clue. Barnabas, whose name was Joseph, was given his adopted name in the Hebrew as *Bar Nabba*. We find two Hebrew words that are key to knowing his Hebrew name—first *bar* meaning *adopted son* and second *nabiy'* meaning *prophet* or *inspired man*. Barnabas was known to the apostles as "the exhorter," implying a prophet who encourages. The Hebrew people often named their children according to their prophetic destiny. Joseph, or *Bar Nabba*, was now part of the New Covenant family that changed or fulfilled his call (and name) as a prophetic man.

According to biblical scholars, Elisha spent 10-12 years as a servant helper to Elijah before his commissioning in Elijah's stead. During that time, we hear nothing of Elisha's voice as he was in the school of God's making. Interestingly, through that time of preparation, he learned to walk in the prophetic gift before being commissioned into the office. His commissioning came at the time of Elijah's ascension into the heavens. After Elisha's commission, he was given the responsibility of training sons or a group of prophets while living out his divine purpose in God. Elisha ministered in the office of a prophet and also equipped other sons of the prophets (see 2 Kings:1, 2).

Jesus is the full incarnation of God as an apostle, prophet, evangelist, pastor (shepherd), and teacher. Through that incarnation and on the resurrection side of the Cross is where He gave those five ministries (or ascension) gifts to men. He gave them as being a part of His divine nature. It is only through His divine nature (spiritual DNA) that anyone given these ministry gifts can function in true authority that bears the power of His name. In knowing this, we must be aware that the offices mentioned are the eternal call of the Creator. Our life's ministry may be any level of those incarnate functions or a Kingdom governmental office of those gifts. To activate our place in the Body of Christ, God gives us the power to be responsible for the function of that gift or office.

Our having a gift or a governmental office in a prophetic role of being like God's Son is solely by grace and calling. His infinite wisdom will provide for us a place and timing to be equipped for the work of the ministry to which He calls us.

Coming to Maturity

The journey on the road toward maturity in our prophetic calling requires a stop for a time of practical learning. In the Greek language, we find the word *katartismos,* translated *to equip.* The word *equip* in Ephesians 4:12 means *to fit, frame, adjust, to mend, to complete, or to bring to completion, to be fully prepared for service.* One primary function of a New Covenant prophet is to equip the Body of Christ for the work of the prophetic gifts and ministry. Additionally, the New Covenant prophet is to equip all saints to recognize God's voice instead of other voices. Obviously, this is a "God thing," to strengthen the Body and build it on the true foundation, which is Christ.

There are currently several schools of prophecy throughout the US and other countries that are true equipping places. As we learned in the above paragraphs, schools of prophecy should actually mean groups of prophetic people coming together with one purpose. That purpose is to know Him first; then we follow Him because we know His voice through our relationship with Him not only as the great Shepherd but also as Friend and Savior. My intent is not to change the name from "school" to "groups," "sons," or "companies," but to understand a better way to approach the art of hearing and knowing God's voice and then to learn and practice the various ways in which He engages with His prophetic people today. These schools are best staffed with seasoned equippers, often "second generation prophets"

Chapter 2 - Comprehending Prophecy

who were mentored by the fathers of the prophetic reformation, which began in the early 1980s. These schools should furnish the prophetic student with experience, motivation, activation, and written materials that move them toward a mature prophetic lifestyle.

Christ-like qualities must be resident in those who lead prophetic schools. We look for experienced, mature, leaders who have excellent track records in prophetic ministry. "Experienced" does not mean they have to be internationally known or have led prophetic conferences. We look for significant activity, character, and likeness of Jesus the prophet through a lifestyle and history of loving the Lord's Body. These individuals should have also reproduced their gift by calling in other prophetic people. Having accountability in all areas of their life, including marriage, finances, ministry, and citizenship is important.

The advancement of the prophetic student is the goal leading them to know and hear God more clearly for themselves and others—not just to become a prophet. There should be sound academic and biblical studies along with character building and practical workshops that apply what they have learned. Protocol and administration of prophecy are also a primary part of the student's growth.

Prophecy is conveying the heart of God to His people through the voice of those who have the revelatory *gifts* of the Spirit. These revelatory gifts reveal to us something of the heart, mind, and purposes of God for personal and Kingdom application, knowledge, and wisdom beyond what that which the Scriptures may reveal. These gifts include a word of knowledge, a word of wisdom, prophecy, and the gift of discerning of spirits. We could also add the gift of tongues and the interpretation of tongues when given as a prophetic utterance. Those particular gifts are a part of prophetic speaking for individuals, local church bodies and regions with a national and international Kingdom emphasis.

A Paradigm Shift of Prophetic Revelation

Beginning Words

What we may term as common or personal prophecy is outlined in 1 Corinthians 14:1-5. Verse 3 gives us the heart of God for this speaking. Those who prophesy in this manner build up, encourage, and bring confident comfort to the hearers. It often confirms God's heart for the individual or corporate entity on any occasion. Simple prophecy will never leave the recipients confused, discouraged or in despair. God purposed this gift to inspire, encourage, strengthen, bring peace, joy, and call to our attention His heart of love for us (see 1 Corinthians 13:1-2) We will give deeper definition to these terms in Chapter 6 of this book.

One thing of prime importance in the equipping of prophecy that every student needs to understand is that we all begin with the basics of hearing and knowing God's voice. If we do not understand and know the voice of God, then we will most likely misrepresent His intent of speaking to us. The prophetic speaker releases what the Spirit says as spoken, prayed, or sung to those who receive. In my early years of acknowledging the voice of God, I had no understanding of how, when, or to whom I was to share what the Lord was showing and speaking to me. Because I lacked in being equipped (there were no places of prophetic equipping in those years), I made many mistakes in expressing what I was hearing or seeing in the spiritual realm. Dreams and supernatural experiences were not the norms for churches I was involved with in the 1960s. I was misunderstood and did misrepresent God's heart at various times. When I heard about the equipping ministries, I suddenly realized why prophecy was so easily abused and misused without the process of being taught and mentored.

In this covenant, unlike the Old Covenant, God's Spirit resides in every believer. Therefore, we all have the capability to hear His voice. But we must also remember that not all are prophets, but all may prophesy in simple prophecy. We are all sheep led by Jesus, the Good Shepherd, to the food, water, and protection of God. He spoke clearly about His intent for us to hear his voice in John 10:3-4:

Chapter 2 - Comprehending Prophecy

*To him the doorkeeper opens, and the sheep hear his voice; and **he calls his own sheep by name** and leads them out. And when he brings out his own sheep, he goes before them; and **the sheep follow him because they know his voice**.*

All believers in Christ can hear His voice and, yes, He speaks to us through Scripture, which is the written Word. My point is that He speaks of hearing ***His voice*** and that He knows us by name, which is where the prophetic is designed to speak to specifics in addition to our general understanding of God from His written Word. God shows His intent for kinship with us desiring to develop a Father/son relationship. The relationship is one of the most vital parts of Kingdom living for the prophetic person. It is in our relationship that we begin to love and understand the intent and heart of God for ourselves and others prophetically.

In the equipping process, we learn His voice and character by practicing love, quietness, hiddenness, humility, and experiencing His presence. Paul makes this clear as he writes to the Corinthians *"Pursue love, and desire spiritual gifts, but especially that you may prophesy"* (1 Corinthians 14:1). I can honestly say that God's love in my prophetic life has brought His love to those whom I have prophesied to. Over the last 25 years, I have watched un-equipped and ill-equipped prophetic people stumble over the need to be trained and mentored because of not clearly knowing His voice. They have heard the call but missed the vitally required training by those God has set in the Body for that purpose.

I recall a student in my prophetic I class who had an attitude that she already knew how to prophesy and was just in the class to practice what she knew. She was disruptive and found it difficult to follow protocol and enter into the teamwork of the class. Her first written assignment was arrogant and rude toward the author who had over 25 years of experience and was recognized internationally as a prophet in the Body of Christ. She was what I would call ill-equipped, thinking she had already finished the course. This young woman showed up for most of the 8-week course, but received an incomplete for refusing to do the required reading. Her evaluation at the end of the class was poor and she received a recommendation to take the class again, which she did not.

In the same class was a young man with an Evangelical background who wanted to know about the gifts and specifically prophecy. He came for a different reason than the young woman. He excelled in the class and went on to take the Prophetic II class. He also asked me to mentor him, which I did for over a year. He and his wife now lead a youth ministry where they teach them how to hear God's voice and to prophesy. He saw the need for equipping, received it, and will surpass me in due time.

Some believe that prophecy is better caught than taught! However, one must have first received the gift by the Holy Spirit before growth and development begin. Without equipping, people find themselves copying the only model they have ever known, often adopting the Old Covenant style from the reading of Scripture. In some circles, there has been no New Covenant approach to prophetic equipping, and, therefore, they can only operate under a partial understanding of the gift of prophecy.

If Jesus had just imparted a gift to the disciples and said "you're on your own; work it out," there would have been little active power, love, discipline, or glory given to God. In truth, there would have been a mess. So He equipped these first apostles through demonstration, love, and practical application. Did they make messes? Yes. But He was always there to help them clean it up through loving correction.

Later, after His resurrection and ascension, He gave gifts to men and called those he nurtured, mentored, and equipped to equip others for the work of the ministry (see Ephesians 4:11-16). The 12 apostles were the first to equip because they had been equipped and empowered to do the work. They lived in the very nature, character, and likeness of Jesus. All equipping ministries must have this attitude. Not that they have a title of apostle, prophet, evangelist, pastor, or teacher but that they live a lifestyle of the very character, nature, and likeness of God's Son.

Chapter 2 - Comprehending Prophecy

The Works of Prophecy

In the New Covenant writings, the prophetic gift is working primarily with Peter, John, Silas, Barnabas, Agabus, and Paul. The apostle Paul writes in Ephesians 4:11:

> *And He Himself gave some to be apostles, some prophets, some evangelists, and some pastors and teachers, for the equipping of the saints, for the work of the ministry, for the edifying of the Body of Christ.*

Based on the above writing, we realize that there are five specific equipping ministries in the Body of Christ. God's will for the church, then, is the acceptance of the prophet as an equipping ministry among their other responsibilities.

We must also glean from Scripture the different functions in the role of prophecy and prophetic ministry. In doing this, we can comprehend the various ways in which the Body can move in prophecy. In Acts 21:8-11, we find prophecy practiced on different levels:

> *On the next day, we who were Paul's companions departed and came to Caesarea, and entered the house of Philip the evangelist, who was one of the seven and stayed with him. Now this man had four virgin daughters who prophesied. And as we stayed many days, a certain prophet named Agabus came down from Judea.*

First, we find that Philip, an evangelist, had four daughters who prophesied. The gift of simple prophecy for edification, exhortation, and comfort is revealed in Philip's daughters. A few days before Paul arrived in Caesarea, he had visited other disciples in Tyre. There, they told him by the Spirit not to go to Jerusalem. Here, Paul was given a personal directive word from these disciples about his journey. In this exhortation, we find that all may prophesy, but not all are

A Paradigm Shift of Prophetic Revelation

prophets. So, as Paul and his companions now find their place in Caesarea, he has a divine appointment with Philip's four daughters who prophesy. It may be significant here that these four daughters prophesied in confirming the word previously received from those at Tyre concerning Jerusalem. This may sound speculative on my part, but through our journeys to different lands, we received similar words of prophecy about our final destination. One of the reasons God uses this gift is for confirmation of the direction He is leading. Perhaps the prophecy from the disciples at Tyre was that Paul was not to go immediately to Jerusalem but to wait for further instructions from the Lord. It was evident due to the course of his journey that he believed he was to go to Jerusalem. I believe it was not by coincidence that Paul went to Philip's house where there resided four prophetic daughters.

Next, a prophet named Agabus shows up from Judea. Why would he need to come to Philip's house when there were already four young women who prophesied? It seems the Lord wanted to take this prophecy to another level, and so He sends Agabus, a prophet, to Caesarea. It was quite a long journey from Judea to Caesarea in those days, so Agabus had some time to ponder the prophetic word the Lord had given him for Paul. Interestingly, Agabus focused on Paul's belt, conveniently found in Philip's house. When Agabus shows up, he immediately takes Paul's belt and binds his own hands and feet, and states, *"Thus says the Holy Spirit, 'So shall the Jews at Jerusalem bind the man who owns this belt, and deliver him into the hands of the Gentiles'"* (Acts 21:11).

This is so vital for us to see as we proceed in developing our prophetic gift. Those with the simple gift of prophecy have authority for general confirming and encouraging words while those in the office of a prophet have authority with greater responsibility in the Kingdom. The saints with the gift of prophecy gave Paul the first words, perhaps confirmed by Philip's four daughters, and later, Agabus gives the details and warnings of what will happen to Paul in Jerusalem. We find that Agabus has a proven ministry as he is

Chapter 2 - Comprehending Prophecy

mentioned earlier in Acts Chapter 11 as one of the prophets from Jerusalem who gave warning of a coming plague in the land.

Paul as the recipient of all these words had to weigh and judge them as he writes in 1 Corinthians 14:29. He had now received several words about Jerusalem. I suggest that the first words from those in Tyre were, to Paul, very general. But being a man filled with the wisdom of God, he considered them. Next, he comes to Philip's house in Caesarea where four young women have the gift of prophecy. I believe this may have more significance in Scripture than we have realized. Firstly, that according to Peter's interpretation of the outpouring of the Holy Spirit at Pentecost, that women would also prophesy. Secondly, I believe the women may have confirmed some things about Jerusalem to Paul before Agabus came on the scene. Finally, I think that final word of Agabus' was easily received by Paul as Agabus was a known prophet in the land at that time. Scripture clearly shows us that Agabus was accountable to the other prophets and leaders in Judea and Jerusalem. Paul, also being in a leadership role, recognized Agabus' authority as a prophet.

My point here is that different levels of prophecy come from the level of responsibility we have in the Body of Christ. We find in 1 Corinthians 12:28, *"And God has set some in the church, first apostles, second prophets, third teachers, etc..."* This is not a hierarchical order but an order of responsibility given by God to those He appointed to His Church. We will further define various prophetic functions in another part of this book.

Finally, we comprehend prophetic gifts and ministry from the Scriptures as well as those who have experienced and practiced it for many years. Some of the problems of past generations in understanding and accepting prophecy have come from our lack of knowing the heart of God. We have put Him in boxes of our own making and whatever we haven't known—out of fear—we have discarded, including many vital gifts given by God for the benefit of the Kingdom. Prophecy and the gifts of the Spirit were never abandoned by God; yet many thought and taught that we moved into an era of

A Paradigm Shift of Prophetic Revelation

some new dispensation of time when God suddenly changed. The Scriptures are clear that *"I am the Lord; I do not change,"* and He is the same yesterday, today, and forever (see Malachi 3:6; Hebrews 13:8). We must choose to let God be God and to know His Word, but of equal importance, to know Him. Only in our relationship with Him do we know Him. Our prayer life must become one of dialogue; our commitment to the Kingdom must be one of a sincere heart and obedience. We must know His voice so that we do not entertain strange voices that lead away from Him. Prophecy is a major key to leading us into greater Kingdom dynamics that agree with the heart, mind, and purposes of God.

Prayer

We give our lives to the fullness of Your intent and pleasure in giving us the prophetic gift. Our desire is to speak only those things that we know to speak through the practice of hearing Your voice. As we live and walk with You, we begin to comprehend the nature and intent of the prophetic gift and our timing and delivery of speaking out so that those who hear our words will also understand the full purpose of prophecy. We know that "the testimony of Jesus is the spirit of prophecy" (Revelation 19:10b).

Chapter 3

Knowing the True

Jesus said to him, "I am the way, the truth and the life. No one comes to the Father except through Me" (John 14:6).

I often hear the same question from both believers and non-believers: "What is truth?" The church has a tendency to worship truths and spiritual experiences that contain truth. Unfortunately, many who say they are followers or believers in Christ see only parts of the biblical truth that fit their agendas, ideas, or concepts of what truth is. In many cases, this question brings on heated debates in the Body of Christ and then suddenly biblical experts are called in to settle the debate, which, in my experience, leaves it up to no more than a coin toss decision. So, what then is truth? True followers of Christ can only come to one conclusion. If we believe what is written in the Word of God, then we believe that all is truth whether it is historical, prophetic, or the Gospel of the Kingdom. If Jesus is the way, the truth, and the life and no one comes to the Father except through Him, then Jesus Himself is the completion or fulfillment of all truth from the beginning of creation.

For prophetic people to prophesy truth, we must have an intimate relationship with the truth always leading to evidence of the truth spoken. The following Scripture came to John the apostle leading him to a greater relationship with the truth. He experienced this while engaged with the Spirit.

A Paradigm Shift of Prophetic Revelation

> *Then he said to me, write: "Blessed are those who are called to the marriage supper of the Lamb!" And he said to me,* ***"These are the true sayings of God."*** *And I fell at his feet to worship him. But he said to me, "See that you do not do that! I am your fellow servant, and of your brethren who have the testimony of Jesus, worship God! For the testimony of Jesus is the spirit of prophecy" (Revelation 19:9-10, emphasis mine).*

Prophecies contained in the Word of God are ***the true sayings of God.*** We know and can testify of the biblical prophecies fulfilled, and we wait on the timing of those not yet fulfilled because we receive the truth by studying, abiding, and living in Jesus who is the truth.

Jesus proclaimed to Phillip the following: *"He who has seen Me has seen the Father; so how can you say, 'Show us the Father'"?* (see John 14:9)—the Father being God as Jesus and the Holy Spirit are also God—being One in the same likeness, nature, character, and purpose. My point here is this: Jesus is the truth of God who came in the flesh as the Living Word of whom the apostles heard, looked upon and handled, concerning the Word of Life (see 1 John: 1-5; see also John 1:14, 17). For a prophetic person to prophesy, that is to speak for the God of the Word, we must first know the Word of God. Prophetic speakers must not only have more than a working knowledge of God's Word but have a relationship with the God of the Word.

Our knowing and studying the written Word must be a significant part of our spiritual relationship with the Godhead. Included in this relationship is the art of conversation in prayer. Prayer is more than a monologue with our God. It is a dialogue with Him. In dialogue, both parties speak and listen. When such a conversation takes place, trust in the relationship is built and love is manifest. Love is a command of Jesus to the believer:

> *"A new commandment I give to you, that you love one another, as I have loved you, that you also love one another" (John 13:34; see also John 14:15-17).*

Chapter 3 - Knowing the True

The Son of God is the complete truth of God. *"If you abide in My word, you are My disciples indeed. And you shall know the truth, and the truth shall make you free"* (John 8:31b-32). Jesus is the One who sets us free to know the truth of heaven on earth. He is the completion of God in us for our purpose on this side of eternity here on earth. How many of us can say that with a deep conviction of knowing the truth of the Gospel of the Kingdom?

The religious spirit in the church closes the gates of heaven to the move of the Holy Spirit in some of our post-modern churches. Most opposition stems from our religious attitudes about who God is and our adopted biblical doctrines. We often hear the term of putting "God in a box," which leads to control, manipulation, and legalism. Thus, we put our Creator in a place of our controlling what He has said or desires to speak! Prophetic gifts and ministries are often the recipients of this kind of opposition since the Old Covenant times. The prophetic voice is given to man as a way for us to know God's heart and intent for His creation. Scripture was written to reveal His heart to His people who were seeking a deeper love and desire to know and serve Him. We have recorded Scripture because God trusted those He had a relationship with to write what he spoke to them. Someone was seeking, abiding, loving, listening, and writing!

Moses, the prophet, received revelation from God and was the author of the first five books of the Bible, which our Jewish brothers call the Torah. Torah means the teachings of Moses—not the Law of Moses. Where did he get these teachings? He received them through his relationship with the Godhead. This portion of Scripture is described as the teaching of Moses because he not only wrote it, but he taught and lived it. Some have defined the Torah as a body of prophetic teaching. Peter writes, *"for prophecy never came by the will of man, but holy men of God spoke as they were moved by the Holy Spirit"* (2 Peter 1:21). Much of the church today considers only the biblical prophets and other biblical characters as holy men or women of God. Therein lies our identity problem and it is a deterrent to the growth of prophecy and the church.

A Paradigm Shift of Prophetic Revelation

The apostle John gives the description of holiness as he writes about the purposes of the Holy Spirit. As John writes his book of the gospel, he reiterates the relationship of Christ and the Holy Spirit, and our relationship with them. One profound statement John makes is that the Spirit will not only be with us but will dwell (have His life) in us. Through the sacrificial blood of Christ and the infilling of the Holy Spirit, we begin living a life of holiness to the Lord. We are conformed daily to the very image and likeness of Christ as sons of God. Our spirits are holy and our soul and body are being changed daily by responding to the Spirit of Holiness in us! As prophetic people we must take on this true identity because it is God's intent that we be holy as He is holy (see Leviticus 20:7; 1 Peter 1:15)! So, we also become holy by living a Christ-like lifestyle. As men and women of holiness, our prophetic words will be of the divine nature.

Some biblical scholars describe holiness as splendid, pure, and untarnished. Scripture teaches us that we are partakers of Christ in the divine nature. In that life, God's nature comes through the sovereign acts of power released to us through the Holy Spirit. Thus, living a godly life comes through our knowing Him relationally not just knowing about Him. It is vital that we embrace and allow our Father and God to live His life in us and release it into the atmospheres in which we live. Our prophetic lifestyles are lived out by the promises He grants concerning our life and godliness. Those promises are the attributes of godly character such as moral excellence, knowledge (knowing God), self-control, perseverance, godliness, brotherly kindness, and love (see 2 Peter 1:3-11). Holiness is a dynamic of absolute godly excellence in living a prophetic lifestyle personally and as the church. It is not something we learn; it is something we become through our relationship with the Holy God. Holiness must first be lived in Him before it can indeed be released as Him. If we who are in prophetic ministry would press into and live the godly attributes of the divine nature, our prophecies would be more of Him and less of us.

Interestingly, the early church was primarily Hebrew for the first 10 years. They understood holiness to the Lord and that they were called to be a kingdom of priests on the earth. The early church, which included the prophets Agabus, Judas, Silas, Barnabas, and the apostle Paul, lived a holy lifestyle to God in Christ.

The Beginning

In the beginning, mankind was created in the image of the Godhead. It was in that image that the relationship with God and man is defined. God walked with Adam, and they conversed in the Garden about the things that were on His heart for the creation. God's man then began co-laboring with Him in the creative and spiritual realm and was given authority over the things on the earth. God desired to reproduce Himself through mankind, and it was His intent to do that. We were created (in the pre-Adamic fall) to have a "life in the Garden" relationship with our Creator in the eternal realm of His being. The eternal realm is simply this—"life in the absolute sense, life as God has it, that which He gave to the Incarnate Son to have in Himself" (see Vine's Complete Expository Dictionary). Mankind was to live and walk in the presence of God! What does that mean? An Israeli friend gave me a definition of God's name, YHVH, in Hebrew. She examined every Hebrew letter of His name and found the root of every letter and the past, present, and future tense of those letters. The final results of His name should prompt us never to put Him in a box again. YHVH is the living, becoming, present presence that is endless. Because God desired a relationship with mankind, the creation was given for our origin and purpose. We hear God's voice because He alone is the present, presence (forever) becoming, and life that is endless. The apostle Paul wrote

> *And he has made **from one blood** every nation of men to dwell on the earth, and has determined their pre-appointed times and the boundaries of their dwellings, so that they should seek the Lord, in the hope that they might grope for Him and find Him, though he is not far from each of us; for*

A Paradigm Shift of Prophetic Revelation

in Him we live and move and have our being, as also some of your own poets have said, "For we are also His offspring" (Acts 17:26-28, emphasis added).

This has supreme prophetic significance as we move forward in God to reconcile all men to Himself through Christ.

Resistance to these realities of God and the prophetic remain today. Since the beginning of the post-modern prophetic move in the early 1980's, there has been an opposition that stems from lacking knowledge of the heart and purpose of God in prophecy. Much animosity came through teaching about the false before knowing the true. It is tough for us to teach about something being false if we have never seen or known the true. We have over the years stuffed ourselves with learning about God but lacked in actually having a living relationship with Him. There are, of course, conditions in our relationship with God although His love for us is continuous. God chose a people for Himself, instructed them in prophecy and its use, and even brought them redemption through the sacrifice of the Son of His love. And though the Church was primarily Jewish for the first ten years after Jesus' resurrection, he loved and had a plan for the Gentiles deep in His heart.

Do Not Be Ignorant

The Gentile church at Corinth was a zealous church that loved God. Gentiles came into the Kingdom through Christ just as the Jews did after Pentecost. They had the *gifts* of the Holy Spirit but lacked in knowledge of the proper purpose and use of them. The apostle wrote to all Christians, not just the early church, pleading, *"But brothers I do not want you to go on being ignorant about the things of the Spirit"* (1 Corinthians 12:1 CJB). For any leader to write or speak such a thing to the Church today would be considered inappropriate. However, this statement of the apostle Paul is as valid and as needed today as it was for the believers at Corinth.

Chapter 3 - Knowing the True

Why would Paul write such a thing to a seemingly prosperous and growing church? The Corinthian church had received and embraced the *gifts* of the Spirit but lacked in knowledge of their proper use. In those days, the things of the Spirit were a part of being a believer. Evidently, because they lacked proper training and oversight, Paul found them to be without order and protocol. Their services were disrupted due to improper protocol and use of the *gifts*. Paul, as an apostolic father, proclaimed their activity in the *gifts* as ignorant and through his letter to them, he gave answers to solve the problems that occurred. God is a God of order and structure who has given us grace for freedom in the things of the Spirit. Freedom is built upon the proper protocol and structure of the applicable disciplines of the gifts.

Much of today's Church has similar problems that must be addressed and corrected. One reason these problems occur is due to our lack of responsible oversight. Accountable oversight of prophecy is best given by seasoned prophetic ministers as part of a team consisting of the other ministry gifts. Leaders who want to embrace prophecy should build relationships with prophetic ministers they know and trust. Without proper oversight and training, leaders who know about and embrace the prophetic *gifts* find themselves in a dilemma simply because they assume God will take care of things, and those they appoint will understand the proper protocol and operation of the *gifts*. This mistake comes from a heart that would like to see everyone involved with what God gives. Somehow, through unsanctified mercy or grace, a program is set up by trusted members without the training and oversight of a seasoned prophetic minister. Often there is no program at all, and prophecy becomes a free for all. Suddenly, someone inexperienced gives an off-the-wall word that is not for edification, exhortation, or comfort. Thinking these things are okay, others follow suit and a complete mess occurs, causing prophecy to be shut down due to lack of proper instruction and fathered oversight. When this takes place in a larger, more popular church, where many visitors come, a whole city or region can be adversely affected.

A Paradigm Shift of Prophetic Revelation

It seems that correction to problems with the gifts of the Holy Spirit or any other controversial subject brings embarrassment to most leaders in the Body. True correction must come from those who can speak the truth in love. We must seek out those ministries who have proven experience, integrity, and love for the Body of Christ to help us solve the problems at hand.

Because the Holy Spirit continues to distribute the gifts to us, He will also provide those to properly equip us in their use. One characteristic of the Holy Spirit is that whatever He does will always glorify Christ! So if messes are made with a gift He has given, it is because of our own immaturity. God gave us the ministry gifts to help bring us to maturity. I love what the apostle wrote in 1 Corinthians 14:1: *"Pursue love, and desire spiritual gifts, but especially that you may prophesy."* With love as the primary importance, prophecy has the emphasis to encourage, strengthen, and bring well-being to the Body of Christ. Perhaps in our times of meditating on God and Scripture, we should consider the above as part of that time.

How can we continue in ignorance of the gifts when the apostle Paul has written simple, loving instructions for the proper use of prophecy and the other gifts? With that thought in mind, we must see the prominence of God's Kingdom heart in the current time. When the Lord restores a gift such as prophecy, it is because He wills to use that gift to advance the Kingdom. For us to be in agreement with His purposes, we must take all He has provided for the restoration and move forward in the wisdom of God.

According to the apostle's writing, prophecy and the revelatory *gifts* are an important part of the Body for Kingdom function. If we read 1 Corinthians, Chapter 12 in its entirety, we find that all the gifts are given the analogy of being a part of the whole purpose of God. Just as a physical body is handicapped when one part is cut off, so when one of the gifts of the Spirit is not functioning in the church, that "body" is also handicapped. Such has been the case in much of the Church today because they are becoming lovers of pleasures rather than lovers of God. When we deny the use of the gifts because of fear, then we become those who have a form of godliness but deny His power. Denying God's power through fear of the gifts handicaps the full intent and power of God in advancing His Kingdom. The *gifts* of the Spirit are power tools for Kingdom advancement. The true power of God is in His love. So use of the tools without God's love is having only a form of godliness. The Church can no longer operate in this manner but instead must embrace all that God has given us to exalt His glory! If we are to advance the Kingdom of God, then we must move forward in all that He is and has freely given us.

Advancing the Kingdom

Now is the time for the Body of Christ to engage individually and corporately for the advancement of the Kingdom. In Peter's interpretation of the outpouring at Pentecost, a flood of revelation came to God's people for Kingdom advancement. He saw a wave of power and authority transform everyone in the Kingdom, empowering them to experience a vital part in victory. Some refer to this outpouring as Joel's army. In order for an army to have confident victory, it must use all resources, training, and insight given by the Commander in Chief. In such an army, no one can attempt to break rank because all know their positions and are fully ready and able to stand and advance until victory is obtained. This will require of us no less than complete commitment to the call and equipping of the saints.

Prophecy plays a vital role in the future of the Kingdom. Each soldier will now be able to hear God's voice for their part in victorious Kingdom living. Forward motion will be assured as they live by protocol, position, and authority. This army will be trained so if a fellow soldier falls in the battle, they will be immediately replaced. It is the responsibility and calling of specific prophetic ministries to equip us in that discipline. While other prophetic ministries will have different assignments and offices, God will provide us with those to equip us.

A Paradigm Shift of Prophetic Revelation

The Kingdom will go forward because we will no longer focus on the enemy's false power but on the victorious Commander who dwells within us. He does not retreat! We will know the voice of the Good Shepherd Jesus so well that strange voices will not be commonplace. To identify the false and deal with it, we must live in the truth. The truth is the person of Jesus Christ who dwells in the believer.

We only have the counterfeit because there is something to be copied or mimicked from the true. It is vital and important to have a living relationship with the Living God. When we have this, we are equipped and able to identify the false and deal accordingly.

Just as we have genuine and false prophetic ministry or prophecy, we cannot have false prophets unless there are true prophets. We have focused on the false for years because we have not known the true. This idea has turned our trust more toward man than God in that the fear of man has been prominent in the knowledge and fear of God. Our churches have feared the voice of men in their alarm against the false, rather than being taught to discern the Spirit of the holiness of God. False prophets and prophecy emerge from the activity of the fear of man. In this same manner of thought, the church has been programmed to react in fear of the unknown rather than to wait, listen, and respond to the known voice of God. React means to act in return or go back to a former position. Respond means to answer, to reply, or to act in return, as if in answer. The nature of true prophetic ministry is to respond to a reply to what God is doing in the situation, even if fear is the ensuing spirit at the time. So do we **react in fear, or respond in faith, trusting God for the solution?**

The Key of Love

The Holy Spirit rains the love of God abroad in our hearts and comforts and brings us into all truth. He is the Spirit of truth sent from the Father who guides us into all truth. He is also the One who distributes the *gifts* as He wills in His union with the Godhead. John writes of the works of the Spirit because he experienced them in Christ and himself. In John Chapter 16, we find astonishing truths about God through the Holy Spirit.

> *However when He, the Spirit of truth has come,* ***He will guide you into all truth;*** *for He will not speak on his own authority, but* ***whatever He hears He will speak*** *and* ***He will tell you things to come.*** *He will glorify Me, for* ***He will take of what is Mine and declare it to you. All things that the Father has are Mine.*** *Therefore I said that* ***He will take of Mine and declare it to you*** *(John 16:13-15, emphasis added).*

In verses 13-15, we find deep revelation that will help us in our prophetic gift of knowing God's voice. This portion of Scripture has helped me and many others move in confident faith in knowing God's voice in prophecy and personal issues of life. First, because the Holy Spirit dwells within us, **He guides us into all truth**. He is One with the Godhead and **never speaks on His Own authority** because **He only speaks of the sovereign council of the Father and the Son.** And when He does speak, He will also **show us things to come.** Thus, the will of God to speak to us through **the indwelling Spirit is present and future tense.** I believe and have experienced the wisdom of God to reveal things of the past in order to help us understand the current and future Kingdom destinies. This should build confidence in our knowing that we are complete in Him. Additionally, Jesus states that **everything the Spirit says to us will glorify Him** and further, the **Holy Spirit will take of all that Jesus has in the Father and declare that to us!** The Lord continues to expound the depth of God's will in saying that **all things the Father has are His and therefore the Holy Spirit will take of those things and declare them to us.** How much of God do we desire to know? There are no limits! What a profound statement of God's intent for us to know and hear His voice through the indwelling Holy Spirit. This is a simple but extremely powerful promise that we must embrace by faith and practice daily in our relationship with the Father.

Accordingly, there are no limits to the knowledge of God in our relationship with Him. By knowledge, I mean in our knowing Him through an intimate and active relationship. There is a Hebrew word, *da'ath*, which implies knowing God and His intent for us rather than knowing about Him. In the Greek, the word *epignosis* describes exact and full knowledge similar in meaning as the intimacy of oneness between husband and wife. Both words imply deep, intimate relationship! When prophetic people build this relationship we build a trust for God because of our intimate love for Him. **Intimate love is reciprocal in that both parties give and receive in an equal measure. We come to know more about a person as we spend time with them.** The Holy Spirit is sent to dwell in us in order to move us toward that deep relationship with the Godhead. For the prophetic person to bring edification, exhortation, and comfort to the Body, we must pursue that kind of love with the Lord in all aspects of life so that this vital *gift* will bring life to those who struggle. Prophecy without the love relationship with God will just be cluttered noise and mumblings.

Dealing with False Prophecy

Although we find ourselves exiting the Old Covenant style of prophecy, we need to embrace the written instruction that remains valid for us today. Moses was the first man chosen by God to help us deal with false prophets and false prophecy. Through his writings in Deuteronomy 13:1-5, the Lord gives us instruction for recognizing false prophecy. In observing the understanding of what is written here, we must remember that the hearers were not filled with the Holy Spirit. Initially, Moses writes that there will arise among us prophets and dreamers of dreams and they will have power to bring a sign and wonder. Interestingly, he puts the two (prophets and dreamers) in the same category. This does not mean that only false prophets have power. He directs us toward knowing the fruit of the false message will be false signs and wonders which will have

CHAPTER 3 - KNOWING THE TRUE

the power to point us to the worship of other gods. We are further instructed not to listen to or entertain that kind of message. Why? Because we know that God has commanded us to love Him with all our heart and with all our soul. Loving God was the issue then and now! If we know and love God through intimate relationship, we have the power to recognize and resist any false prophet or prophecy. Verse 3 in Deuteronomy 13 is clear in stating our stand:

> *...you shall not listen to the words of that prophet or that dreamer of dreams,* **for the Lord YOUR God is testing YOU to know whether YOU love the Lord YOUR God with all YOUR heart and with all YOUR soul** *(emphasis added).*

Therefore, concerning false prophets and false prophecy, God is testing our trust in the covenant and intimate relationship we have with Him. Jesus said that those who "love Me have My commandments," adding that the Father loves us and Jesus will manifest Himself to us! (see John 14:21). We cannot separate the love that God has toward the Body only to this covenant. It was God's intent from the beginning. All true prophetic ministries must have their roots in the love of God to us and in us. God's love in the prophetic person is the power source that forms and releases the words of prophecy from our mouths that are accurate and pure.

The words or actions of false prophets and prophecy will fall to the ground because there is no real authority or love of God in them. False prophecy today is dealt with through the fruit of true prophecy in the Lord's Body. The fruit of the Spirit does not spoil but brings life and nourishment to those receiving it (see Galatians 5:22-25). False fruit comes from a corrupt, tarnished, impure, unjust, deceptive spirit. False fruit spoils, smells bad, and deteriorates. Often when I hear false or immature prophecy it is like getting stabbed in the heart. It affects the senses like that of being betrayed by someone you trusted. Jesus stated this about false prophets *"Beware of false prophets, who come to you in sheep's clothing, but inwardly they are*

A Paradigm Shift of Prophetic Revelation

ravenous wolves" (Matthew 7:15). Ravenous wolves go after the weak, the crippled, the young, and those who stray from the flock. He also talks about knowing them by their fruits: *"You will know them by their fruits. Do men gather grapes from thorn bushes or figs from thistles?"* (see Matthew 7:16.) Think about it. Can one swallow a grape born from a bush of thorns or in like manner a fig that bears thistles? No, they would be difficult to chew on let alone swallow into one's digestive system. That is why I made the comment above about being stabbed in the heart or being betrayed. Those are things that are difficult to deal with and hard to swallow.

Truth has put the false to death through the redemptive blood of Jesus. The truth is easy to receive and brings with it the peace which passes all understanding. True authority and prophecy will produce the fruit of the Spirit. Real authority is not a gift, but comes through an intimate relationship with the one having authority—that is, Jesus (see Matthew 28:18-20.) As stated earlier, when the Holy Spirit speaks, He speaks only what He hears from the Godhead.

It is vital for the prophetic person today to be discipled, equipped, and mentored before being released into active personal or public ministry. In that time of spiritual growth, we move toward maturity like the prophet Samuel and the Lord Jesus, *"So Samuel grew, and the Lord was with him and let none of his words fall to the ground"* (1 Samuel 3:19). Interestingly, Jesus' life was blessed in similar ways as Samuel. *"So when they performed all things according to the law of the Lord, they returned to Galilee, to their own city, Nazareth. And the child grew and became strong in spirit, filled with wisdom, and the grace of God was upon him"* (Luke 2:39-40). Even Jesus had a time to grow naturally and spiritually. He was not released into His ministry by the Father until He was ready. Samuel was not released into his ministry until he grew naturally and in the Lord spiritually. We should never presume that because we have received a gift of prophecy that we are a prophet or ready to minister prophetically.

Presumption carries the traits of being prideful, rebellious, arrogant, and rude. In Deuteronomy 18:20, Moses writes of a

Chapter 3 - Knowing the True

prophetic person who presumes to speak a word in God's name that is not commanded by Him. In this covenant that presumptuous prophet is tested by the truth, showing his words have no power to override God's Kingdom dynamics. The false is exposed and destroyed by the true. We know the true by having His life in us and through our continuous intimacy with Him. As prophetic people, we must grow in the Lord so that our words will not fall to the ground (see my book *The Face of Prophecy – Determining the Truth*).

Finally, in knowing, loving, and living in Jesus the Truth, all prophecy must still be judged. Chapter 8 of this book is dedicated to judging prophecy. Part of being equipped in prophecy should include the wisdom of God in judging prophecy. We should test all things and hold fast to that which is good (see 1 Thessalonians 5:21). Knowing the true is a key to proper prophecy, healthier churches, and moving us into Kingdom authority. If we know the truth of who Jesus is, we will know that which is good, because everything else is in subjection to the "Truth."

Prayer

Thank You for teaching us that Your truth is in the person, nature, love, and character of Your Son Jesus Christ. As Your life infuses and changes ours to be as You are, may we live, love, and prophesy only the truth that is in You. Because as You are, Lord, so are we in this world. Lord, our purpose in speaking prophetically is to release words that are spirit and life.
Amen

A Paradigm Shift of Prophetic Revelation

Chapter 4

New Covenant Prophecy

"Behold the days are coming," says the Lord, "that I will make a new covenant with the house of Israel and the house of Judah – not according to the covenant that I made with their fathers in the day that I took them out of the land of Egypt, My covenant which they broke, though I was a husband to them, says the Lord. But this is the covenant that I will make with the house of Israel after those days, says the Lord: I will put My law in their minds and write it on their hearts; and I will be their God, and they shall be My people" (Jeremiah 31:31-34).

In Jeremiah 31:31-34 the Lord promises His people Israel a New (or renewed) Covenant, unlike the one they continued to break. All who believe in Jesus are now part of the New Covenant and the commonwealth of Israel. Paul writes to the church at Ephesus saying,

…you are no longer strangers and foreigners, but fellow citizens with the saints and members of the household of God, having been built on the foundation of the apostles and prophets, Jesus Christ Himself being the chief cornerstone, in whom the whole building, being fitted together, grows into a holy temple in the Lord, in whom you also are being built together a dwelling place of God in the Spirit (Ephesians 2:19-22).

A Paradigm Shift of Prophetic Revelation

In this Covenant, we no longer prophesy about Him who is to come, but we prophesy in Him who has come, and is the One now seated at the right hand of the Father. To be "in Him" is to be as Him. We who believe in Jesus Christ are conformed to one image, and that is the life and likeness of Him (see John 14:12; Romans 8:29).

We now prophesy in Christ because we are one with Him and the Father. Paul makes it clear that it is not the believer who lives, but the living Christ in us who is now our new life (see John 17:20-23; Galatians 2:20; Colossians 3:3). Our identity is not in our gift, vocation, or profession but is entirely in Christ and therefore we prophesy in Him as a part of His Body. Our gift is the Holy Spirit of God, freely given because of His love and destiny for our lives in His Kingdom. Prophecy then is not about the Old or New Covenant, but Christ in us as the hope of glory.

Some people believe that the apostle Luke made a distinction between the Old Covenant prophets and those of the New Covenant in Luke 16:16. Here, Jesus tells the religious Pharisees that John the Baptist is the last of the Old Covenant prophets. Did this mean that there would be no more prophets in the commonwealth of Israel? No, it only meant that all prophecy would now point to the Kingdom of God, and all the dynamics of heaven would be the same on earth. The Lord released a new breed of prophets, prophetic ministers, and prophecy in the earth. As prophets and prophecy are a function in the Body of Christ, that role will enhance God's intent of the Body toward the heart, mind, and purposes of Himself in advancing His Kingdom.

Jesus said in Matthew 23:34 that He will send prophets, wise men, and scribes. The book of Acts refers to the prophets, Agabus, Judas, Silas, and Barnabas. In Acts Chapter 13, individual prophets and teachers (perhaps prophetic teachers) named Simeon (called Niger), Lucius, and Manaen were a part of the church at Antioch. It is not clear here who the prophets are except they are named among those at Antioch. In 1 Corinthians 12:28 prophets are among those set in the church by God. In 1 Corinthians 14:29-32 the apostle Paul writes of prophets speaking in the local Body. John the beloved, who wrote one of the four gospels and three letters to the church, was obviously a prophet as he recorded the revelation of Christ, which we call the book of Revelation. The book of Ephesians tells us that Jesus, the One who ascended into the heavens, gave gifts to some in the Church to be apostles, prophets, evangelists, pastors, and teachers called to equip us for the work of the ministry. These ministry gifts were given by Christ, *"until we all arrive at the unity implied by trusting and knowing the Son of God, at full manhood, at the standard of maturity set by the Messiah's perfection"* (Ephesians 4:13 CJB).

The above five ministry gifts carry His nature, love, and character. They also carry His life message. There were obviously many prophets in the New Covenant mentioned by implication of the term "prophets" throughout Scripture, although not all are specifically named. Knowing this, it is important for us to understand that titles attached to names in this covenant are not of great importance except for specific incidences in Scripture that build the Kingdom and ensure spiritual growth. Today, we must look for Jesus the prophet in those who prophesy as we now prophesy in Him as a part of the Body of Christ. The New Covenant Church continues to communicate to us through His written word and prophetic ministry.

New Covenant Functions

A primary function often overlooked by the Church is that the New Covenant prophet has the responsibility of equipping the saints for the work of the ministry. Most of the church today puts that total responsibility under the title of the pastor or associate pastor. A primary reason for the Body of Christ being weak is our error of putting too much emphasis on the pastoral position as the absolute authority. He gave us all five ministry gifts to equip the saints for service (see Ephesians 4:11-16). Prophets are often unique in the area of equipping us because God has a history with them. He may have destined them before their birth to be His voice to the Church or nations. He works in them the message for the time in which they live and minister. They have been trained by Him to know, hear, and see in the Spirit so, in turn, they may equip the Church in the ways God speaks through His Spirit abiding in them. Thus, God, in the sovereignty of the Holy Spirit, distributes the things of the Spirit *(gifts)* to whomsoever He wills. Within that distribution of gifts we find different levels of prophetic gifting in the Body of Christ today that help bring the saints to maturity.

New Covenant prophets also function as foundation builders who understand the mysteries of Christ based on the revelation given to them by God concerning building the spiritual house. That house is both the Hebrew and Gentile Church, which is destined to be *one new man*—the fullness of God in His church (see Ephesians 2:14-16). Along with the apostle, the prophet builds the foundation, of which Jesus Christ is the chief cornerstone, upon which all the truth of the church is built in length, depth, width, and height unto a dwelling place of God in the Spirit (see Ephesians 2:19-22). All of this ongoing revelation of the Spirit is given to His apostles and prophets. New Covenant prophecy comes by revelation from the Spirit and will agree with the Gospel of the Kingdom and all that is written in this Covenant. The prophet and all the Body of Christ must be engaged in living in this New Covenant with its better promises (see Hebrews 8:6). The Spirit reveals this authority so that the manifold wisdom of God is made known by the Church to the principalities and powers in heavenly places. The prophet, along with the apostle and teacher, will have a significant revelation by the Holy Spirit that God's intent will be known to principalities and powers in the heavenly places; the varied and multi-colored wisdom of our God living in us, the Kingdom Church. In that knowledge is revealed the real power and authority of God in the spiritual house called His Body, the Church. The above statements are all according to God's eternal purpose accomplished by Jesus through the Cross (see Ephesians 3:1-13).

Another message of the New Covenant prophet is that we are living in the times of restoration of all things that have been spoken

CHAPTER 4 - NEW COVENANT PROPHECY

by the His holy prophets since the world began. The prophetic theme of our time is based on restoration, revelation of our new nature, purifying the church, living in the Spirit, and being "as He is so are we in this world" (see 1 John 4:17). In all this the New Covenant prophet releases the Father's vision of the Church and restores holiness, purpose, and strategy for the advancement of the Kingdom of God on earth as it is in heaven. The emphasis of New Covenant prophecy is the Kingdom of God—Jesus is the King dwelling in us bringing completeness in Him in the fullness of the Godhead bodily (see Colossians 2:9-10).

As I stated previously, prophecy in this Covenant is specifically for building up, encouraging, and bringing well-being to the Body of Christ. Here is the Lord's intent for the Church:

> ...that He would grant you, according to the riches of His glory, to be strengthened with might through His Spirit in the inner man, that Christ may dwell in your hearts through faith; that you, being rooted and grounded in love may be able to comprehend with all saints what is the width and length and depth and height - to know the love of Christ which passes knowledge; that you may be filled with all the fullness of God (Ephesians 3:16-19).

We clearly see here the intention of God for His Son's Body to take back the creation that He in His sovereignty spoke into being for the love and purpose of His pleasure.

The apostle Paul's writings to the Church led the Body into the fullness of God in Christ and them in us. Jesus is the model of the prophetic gift that God has given us for New Covenant prophecy. All prophets, prophetic ministers, and those who prophesy in simple prophecy will have one common thread of emphasis. That is, *"the testimony of Jesus is the spirit of prophecy"* (Revelation 19:10). This simply means that all prophecy in this Covenant will have evidence that Jesus is the Son of God and His emphasis of ministry was that the

A Paradigm Shift of Prophetic Revelation

Kingdom has come to earth! No matter what level those prophecies are given, they will carry the love of God that reveals His nature, character, and likeness for the situation, person/persons, cities, and nations.

Three Categories of Prophecy

Most believers who acknowledge the practice of prophecy as a part of God's Kingdom dynamics agree that there are three distinct levels of prophetic speaking in the New Covenant. Our level of gifting has nothing to do with our importance in the Body. These levels were determined over a period of time through the observation of those who pioneered the present prophetic movement. Where prophecy is currently practiced, we find the three categories practiced are in agreement with the heart of Scripture.

Let's return for a moment to the Old Covenant and see God's intent from that time. In Numbers 11, Moses speaks the heart of God for His people that He desired all of them would be prophets who prophesy. He did not despise the two elders who remained in the camp with the people. The Spirit of the Lord fell upon Eldad and Medad and they prophesied in the camp while all the other elders prophesied with Moses in the tent of meeting. When questioned about this, Moses spoke the heart of God clearly by proclaiming, *"Oh that all the Lord's people were prophets and that He would put His Spirit upon them"* (Numbers 11:29). God desires for us to be His spokesmen in the local body, the national and international church, and in this covenant to the world when applicable. This was His intent from the beginning.

We know from Paul's writing to the Corinthian church that we are to *"pursue love, and desire spiritual gifts, but especially that you may prophesy"* (1 Corinthians 14:1). Later in that same Chapter he states in verse 31 *"that we may all prophesy."* This is a fulfilling of Moses' word to the people of God in Numbers 11. Paul wrote in Chapter 12 that not all are prophets pertaining to the prophetic office. We

Chapter 4 - New Covenant Prophecy

find in Acts Chapter 13 that there were prophets and teachers in the Church at Antioch. Some were sent out so we can assume that some remained in the role of prophetic ministry and equipping the saints of that community.

We find in this Covenant that all may prophesy but that not all are prophets. We need to bring proper understanding of these statements from Scripture to those "wannabe" prophets. When one has a ministry, they serve in the capacity of that ministry. I want to note here that authority in the Kingdom of God is not a gift like the gifts of the Spirit. True authority to use His name in power is established through our relationship with the Godhead. Any authority we are given comes from the level of responsibility that God trusts us with in all things pertaining to Him, His Name, and love. The greater our relationship with God, the greater our authority becomes. Through our relationship with the Godhead, trust is built to carry out the responsibility for the task at hand. An example in the Old Covenant was Joseph's relationship with Pharaoh. As Pharaoh began to trust Joseph through his gift of dream interpretation and servant integrity, Pharaoh released more authority to him.

Not all are called into the office of a prophet or to local and translocal prophetic ministry, but all may prophesy for the purposes of edification, exhortation, and comfort. Prophesying with those specific purposes is the standard for all New Covenant prophecy. We often begin in this level of the *gift* of prophecy that confirms to the hearers something the Holy Spirit may have spoken to them personally at any given time. This wonderful *gift* of prophecy will bring hope, encouragement, and well-being to all recipients. It does not have to be spoken by one in the office or the ministry of a prophet, but any believer who has the prophetic *gift*.

Understanding our level of gifting is vital to the development of our area of ministry. God's heart for us is to grow in character, wisdom, accuracy, and delivery for the common good of the Body. That process of growth will occur in any level of prophetic gifting. Our goal is to arrive, *"at full manhood, at the standard of maturity set by the Messiah's perfection"* (Ephesians 4:13b CJB). These are not required to become a prophet but are character issues for all who prophesy. We are not equipped only by prophets but also by other ministry gifts listed in Ephesians 4:11-12. In all the equipping process, we only prophesy to the degree that the Lord reveals things to us. He will not give us more than we can be trusted with as we grow into the full manhood of Christ.

Prophetically gifted people should realize they can speak in any of the revelatory gifts described in this Chapter. Remember that the Holy Spirit distributes all gifts. To some He gives a word of knowledge, while others release words of encouragement through prophecy. The Lord also gives a combination of gifts. In our zeal to receive *the things of the Spirit,* we must remember that He also gave ministries to equip and nurture us. He provided the prophetic equipping ministry so that we not only speak prophetically to the Body, but also hear Him more clearly for ourselves. The following three categories of prophecy give us a general understanding of how He may distribute the levels of these gifts.

The *Gift* of Prophecy

We must realize that there is no word for *gifts* of the Holy Spirit and in most all Bible translations the word is italicized because it does not exist in the original language of translation. *Pneumatikos* is the word for spiritual or spirituals in the original Greek. This word can be translated as *things of the Spirit,* so when we think of the *gifts* of the Spirit, we are actually referring to that which is of the nature of God, the Holy Spirit. Prophecy is an inspirational flow of the Holy Spirit freely given to a believer for the building up, encouraging, and calming of those receiving from that life flow of the Holy Spirit (see 1 Corinthians 12:7; 10; 14:1). The words of this *spiritual* prophetic flow are often given as personal in nature to those in a local body setting. Often in the nature of this flow of prophecy many receive dreams toward God's will and direction for their own lives (see Acts 2:17-18).

Chapter 4 - New Covenant Prophecy

Prophetic Ministry

In the same manner, we have some in the Body of Christ who are called to a prophetic ministry. This ministry is also given by the Holy Spirit in accordance with the will and purpose of God. I personally believe this could be an Elisha type of experience under the oversight of one who functions as a prophet. We must remember that although Elisha was called by God to be a prophet in Elijah's stead, we do not hear from Elisha for 10-12 years. My point here is *process* through time and God's purpose.

Those called to this ministry will have some of the same functions in the releasing of personal and corporate prophetic words to the local church of which they are a member of the leadership team. Having a prophetic ministry brings with it a use and understanding of words of knowledge, words of wisdom, and the gift of discerning of spirits (see 1 Corinthians 12:7-10). Like others flowing in the Spirit, they will dream dreams and often have an inherent gift of dream interpretation. These people will have a calling by Jesus to function in the ascension gifts (see Ephesians 4:11-12). The prophetic minister will equip in seminars as well as speaking to the local body and leaders about corporate and Kingdom purposes of God. All of this will be done in conjunction with local leaders and one in the office of a prophet.

The Function of the Prophet

This is a specific call and commissioning from the Lord to function as a prophet to the Body of Christ locally, regionally, nationally, and internationally (see Ephesians 4:11-16; 1 Corinthians 12:29-31; 14:29). It is a call of the Lord that is empowered by the Holy Spirit to equip the prophet in inspirational speaking also given to visions, dreams, trances, and words of knowledge and wisdom. The prophet will demonstrate a high level of the gift of discerning of spirits.

A Paradigm Shift of Prophetic Revelation

The New Covenant prophet will build relationship with other leaders and through relationship will be trusted to bring words of correction and/or direction when required. They will also speak to the churches in nations for personal, corporate, and Kingdom issues (see Ephesians 4:11-16; 1 Corinthians 14:31; Ephesians 2:20, 3:5; 1 Samuel 3:20; Daniel 12:4). New Covenant prophets may also become an embodiment of the message they carry. An example would be that of doing prophetic acts such as Agabus picking up Paul's belt in demonstration of the word of the Lord to Paul (see Acts 21:10-14).

The above paragraphs illustrate general parameters of three possible levels of prophetic gifting that vary with the calling, experience and nurturing we receive. We can grow in a greater sphere of our gifting through intimacy with the Lord. A love relationship builds mutual trust that reveals the secrets of the heart. We must pursue the goal of loving Him as He loves us. Our relationship with God is vital for any of these levels of prophetic speaking. Remember our life with God is not about our gifting. The primary goal is to be a mature representative of Christ.

If we are called to prophesy in only one of these levels, we need to understand that it is God's intent that we continue to grow in the anointing and excellence within that level. It is our responsibility to develop the *gifts* which He has given us for Kingdom use, always remembering to give Him the glory and allowing Him to build His nature and character fully into our being.

The Importance of Biblical Standards

Given the above levels of gifting, we need to understand the standards in practicing them. Knowing when, where, why, and how are vital to the practice of prophesying in our measure of authority and responsibility.

Let's consider the practice of prophecy in a local body or small home church scenario. First, the leadership of these groups should be equipped and ready to allow the flow of prophecy as a part of their

Chapter 4 - New Covenant Prophecy

purposes in God. They should set the protocol through knowing the Scriptures and working with an experienced prophetic ministry to help them set it in place and establish through prayer the counsel of God for their meetings. After doing all the above, leaders should announce tthat they have established a protocol for prophetic ministry in their group. It is good practice to have a small brochure or pamphlet for visitors that outlines the protocol for a particular meeting.

On this level of local body prophecy, several things can be done. Some fellowships have an open microphone used for prophetic ministry during the worship. This type of prophecy should be given only for edification, exhortation, and comfort of that local body and given only by those who have been equipped in prophecy. Additionally, good parameters, established by the leadership, should be set in place along with the protocol, for example: no specific direction, correction, or rebukes. The effect of such a protocol will be to encourage the local body and/or specific members in it. This helps promote spiritual growth and love toward the Lord and one another.

Where ongoing training takes place, the leadership should build relationship with those equipped in prophecy. Then, as the Holy Spirit leads the team to engage in prophecy for specific reasons, it can flow from one or more trained people to an individual or group. For example, in our fellowship, I or one of our trained team members may get a word for a visitor or individual we know. At that time, we acknowledge the person or group and begin to prophesy. Often this includes me taking the mic around to other trained individuals who have a prophetic word for those we have acknowledged. These words are always given as confirmation, building up, encouraging and bringing well-being to the recipients. We have seen many people blessed through these types of words over and over as they connect with God's heart for their lives.

Another way ministry can be done in a local body setting is through the development of prophetic teams. We will look at this in depth in Chapter 10 of this book. This takes more time, training, and coordination. First, we have our potential team members go through our eight-week (24-hours total) equipping class. All aspects of prophetic ministry are covered to give them a comprehensive view of the practice of personal prophecy and prophetic ministry. During the eight-week course, we activate the candidates through various workshops and teach them to work as a team of three people—one being an experienced team leader. Once the course is finished, we begin working with those interested in team ministry. The protocol and parameters are very much like those mentioned above.

The Prophetic Minister

Additionally, looking at what I refer to above as prophetic ministry, this is not referring to the office of a prophet but one called to the ministry arena. From my perspective, we require that person to go through another eight-week (24-hours total) course where we deal with character building, prayer, listening, intimacy with God, and the realm of the supernatural in visions, dreams, angelic participation, and working with leadership. Workshops may include practicing listening to God and determining what He is saying to us as a group or for the local body represented by someone in the class. Additionally, we may seek God for words concerning the city or area in which we live as a group. This is demonstrated throughout Scripture as a part of the function of the prophet. These words are recorded, then judged, and then we seek further counsel of the Lord as to the timing and delivery. In the portion about working with leaders, we encourage building servanthood relationship with our leaders. Once this begins, trust and love build the relationship. Examples from Scripture would be that of King David, Gad the seer, and Nathan the prophet, Samuel and Eli, Elijah and Elisha, Paul and Silas at Antioch, and Agabus and the church at Jerusalem.

For those who desire to go further, we offer prophetic mentoring where we meet with the candidates one on one or in small groups, encouraging and helping them progress toward ministry in the local church. Some of these students go on to be involved in their local churches as prophetic ministers, equippers, intercessors, and worshippers.

One role of a prophetic minister in the local church would be working with the pastoral staff as a team member. This person would be one who receives prophetic revelation on a consistent basis. As part of the team, they would work closely in helping that church stay focused on their vision and purpose. Additionally, they would stimulate and stir up other gifts of the Spirit and encourage their use in the church. Some would have a primary emphasis on intimacy and prayer and assist the leadership in the development of those disciplines. Some may even be musicians and prophetic worship leaders. In that aspect, a new freedom of worshipping God would be stirred up, released, and practiced. Any of the above aspects of prophetic ministry can be practiced with oversight by the entire leadership team. Remember, *"Where the Spirit of the Lord is there is liberty"* (2 Corinthians 3:17). We must begin moving in the liberty of God's Spirit in prophetic ministry.

The Prophet Office

Looking at the activities of the New Covenant prophets in Scripture gives us a guideline as to the characteristics of that office today. Agabus was a prophet sent out by the Church at Jerusalem. However, we know there were other prophets in that church because Scripture implies such in Acts 11:27-28. Agabus seemed to have authority from Judea to Antioch. Because we know the five ministry gifts worked as teams, we can assume that the accountability for Agabus was the ministry team in Jerusalem. We can assume the same for Judas and Silas as they were sent out from the council at Jerusalem along with Saul and Barnabas (see Acts 15:22). My point here is that they were part of a local body or council of elders (which could include various ministry office gifts). If they were sent

A Paradigm Shift of Prophetic Revelation

from there, then they were a part of the team or had the primary accountability with that governing body.

This is a model for the church to follow today. What we have termed as "a covering" has become more significantly known as having accountability to others in the Body. The office of a prophet today is similar to the Old Covenant primarily in the ways of hearing and speaking. Today there are some prophets who are part of local body teams and others that may have their accountability to national or regional leadership groups. These prophets may be sent out to minister anywhere the Holy Spirit determines them to go. Many are sent out to minister in large conference settings with a specific Kingdom theme. At times, some prophets who have a relationship with a local body may be called upon to seek the Lord for new direction, purpose, or to just stimulate hope that has been lost. Some are called and sent to equip the saints in prophecy and the hearing and knowing of God's voice. Others may remain as part of a local body team or be sent out as a part of a presbytery team.

A prophet is not a loner wandering about to every church he senses needs correction or a calling back to Covenant obedience. Prophets, like other ministries, are led by the Spirit, not just through invitations from churches or groups. That method may be of God where both parties are hearing from the Lord as to a particular meeting and time frame. We see a model in the New Covenant where most were sent out in teams by the Holy Spirit, prayer, and fasting to bring God's words for regions, people groups, or churches. For the most part, prophets today go to minister as a part of a conference team, regional meeting, or in the context of a Kingdom Council. A prophet plays a significant role as a team member in any of the above venues.

Primarily, prophecy in the New Covenant Church takes on the likeness of being part of the Kingdom focus of God's heart. This gift, ministry, and office know that being part of the Lord's Body must always work as a team with other ministry gifts, churches, and

Chapter 4 - New Covenant Prophecy

regions both nationally and internationally. Prophecy must now take its place in the Body of Christ as an active function to help the church come to maturity in knowing and hearing God's voice. The different levels of the gifting must become as Joel's army, never breaking ranks, because we know our position in moving forward and pressing into the Kingdom.

New Covenant Realities

I believe as of this writing that the prophetic movement in the Church today has only scratched the surface of God's intent. There is an emerging movement among some prophets in the Church today where the ministry of prophecy must take on the face, love, and heart of Jesus. He remains as the head of the Body and without the head, the Body is dead.

In our past history as the church, we have moved from being led by the Spirit into being led by our institutions of higher Christian learning. Scripture tells us *"For as many as are led by the Spirit of God are sons of God"* (Romans 8:14). I have nothing against higher Christian education if it is balanced with the study of Scripture, the Holy Spirit, prayer, and the ministry of Jesus learned and practiced—not only in theory, but in truth and life experiences. Looking at the history of the Church, some universities today began as Schools of Christian Ministry or Theology, but now engage in secular ideas and the false notion that other religions such as Islam, Buddhism, Hinduism, etc. are of the same importance as Christianity. Many of our institutes of higher education teach and believe that the things of the Holy Spirit were for a previous dispensation and God changed them because we now have the Bible.

Today's New Covenant prophetic movement was created by God's Holy Spirit - not an institute of mankind. This movement is now gaining momentum in bringing us back to a position taught in the Scriptures and the practice of prophecy outlined therein for the

Church. I see us moving forward first in the character, nature, and love of God in Jesus. This is of primary importance because the Lord is advancing His Kingdom through the restoration of this marvelous New Covenant ministry of prophets.

Prayer

We believe it is evident in Your Word that we have received from the work of the Cross–a New Covenant with better promises. In that Lord, we declare that our lives and purpose as prophetic people on this earth are to be as it was purposed for us in heaven–now today. We no longer speak as those prophets in the Old Covenant, but now speak in Your Son as sons of this Covenant. Help us to move deeper and further into our purpose as prophetic voices in this Covenant, always glorifying the Son so that You, Father, will be glorified in Him.
Amen

Chapter 5

Contending for Victory

For though we walk in the flesh, we do not war according to the flesh. For the weapons of our warfare are not carnal but mighty in God for pulling down strongholds, casting down arguments and every high thing that exalts itself against the knowledge of God, bringing every thought into captivity to the obedience of Christ, and being ready to punish all disobedience when your obedience is fulfilled (2 Corinthians 10:3-6).

The role of prophecy in spiritual warfare is vital to achieving Kingdom victory in the Body of Christ universally. To understand the current-day role, we must again examine the Old Covenant along with the new. Being a Christian for over 50 years, I have observed and practiced various ways in which the church has engaged the enemy; the Scriptures used and the means in which we have engaged. Some 20 years ago, the Lord revealed to the Body of Christ new strategies and tactics of spiritual warfare. In His grace, He demonstrated that we had often fought exhausting battles already won. Prophetic ministries and intercessors were being alerted by the Holy Spirit that Christians were living a defeated lifestyle unnecessarily. Suddenly, we realized our errors in spiritual warfare.

The apostles wrote concerning our spiritual battles and the indwelling Holy Spirit. In 1 John 3:8 we read *"For this purpose was the Son of God manifested, that He might destroy the works of the*

A Paradigm Shift of Prophetic Revelation

devil." Jesus proclaimed in the gospel of John that *"Most assuredly I say to you, he who believes in Me, the works that I do he will do also; and greater works than these he will do, because I go to My Father"* (John 14:12). These are promises to the New Covenant believer. If He destroyed the works of the devil while here on earth in the form of a man, why do we struggle so as Christians? Just as the prophets of the Old Covenant pointed out Israel's position in the God of our fathers, so shall the prophets today point us to the New Covenant of greater promises (see Hebrews 8:6). The promise in John 14:12 is an act of God's grace that the prophetic ministry must stir us toward proclaiming those works as done in us and through us!

Further, we must hear God about the strategies to stand in the victory Christ gained for us! Such plans are revealed in the Scriptures because what is written is also established concerning the spiritual battles we will face. *"Finally, brethren, be strong in the Lord and the power of His might. Put on the whole armor of God that you may be able to stand against the wiles of the devil"* (Ephesians 6:10-11). Wearing the full armor of God is our first strategy against the wiles (scheming devices) of the enemy directed against us. This Scripture is the legal position of our victory in spiritual warfare. The condition is that we must put on the whole armor of God and wear it daily. Knowing, using, and wearing the full armor is to know our identity in Him *"For you died and your **(real-true)** life is hidden with Christ in God"* (Colossians 3:3, emphasis added; see also Galatians 2:20; Colossians 2:9-10). We find an initial strategy in Colossians 3:3 that our new life in Him is now revealed with Christ in God—the old is hidden and the new exposed as a threat to the enemy. We understand that the old man who died is no longer seen, but the new man revealed in the spiritual realm is our position with Him and in Him as a manifestation of the sons of God. When we truly live in our place of death with Him, then our new life is revealed in us through His power and might.

Another problem concerning the church and spiritual warfare is that a majority of the church has not been educated or activated in the truth of our prominence over the enemy of our souls. Too many in the church have no idea about their positional authority in Christ. Assuring us of our authority comes through an intimate relationship with Him where He trusts us with the authority of His name, character, likeness, and power. The church also lacks in equipping us to stand and live in our position of knowing and living in the promise *"You are of God, little children, and have overcome them, because **He who is in you is greater** than he who is in the world"* (1 John 4:4; see also Romans 8:31-39).

The Father, the Holy Spirit and Jesus live in the believer, making us the living temple of God—the only temple where our God dwells at all times (see 1 Corinthians 6:19 and 2 Corinthians 6:16). The Godhead is not leasing space, but has permanent residence because of our faith and commitment. We have given them the house and through our redemption in Christ's blood, the Father owns the title deed. Satan cannot enter the temple of God, but he can roam about in the outer court influencing the thoughts of those who choose to live in that realm. We are not called to dwell in the outer courts of the temple but rather we dwell in the Holy of Holies as He dwells in us and is the Holy of Holies.

Chasing That Which We Already Have

Often in today's church, we chase after an anointing or manifestation of God's presence in someone else because we have not engaged with the present presence of the indwelling One. If we understand and live all that is written above concerning our position in His death, burial and resurrection, which is our new life, then we will not tend to go after that which we currently possess. However, those we chase after most likely live in the reality of His presence and power in them. An important part of prophetic ministry today is to equip us in the practice of His presence for ourselves, thus turning us back to God and His ways in the New Covenant. Just living in the understanding and keeping of our covenant with God can lead to

A Paradigm Shift of Prophetic Revelation

dominant victory. Our Covenant is the promised new life and new Spirit of the restored position as a son/daughter of God (see also Jeremiah 31:31-34; Ezekiel 36:26-27; Luke 22:20; Romans 11:11, 19; Ephesians 2:11-19). Making us aware of our position of authority in Christ is another part of the prophet's role to equip us for the work of the ministry. Prophets in their relationship with the indwelling One will seek, know, and confirm to us the strategy for victory in our warfare. The Lord reminds us through Timothy's prophetic words to wage the real war by previous prophetic words given to him by the presbytery. We will discuss this in detail later in this Chapter (see 1 Timothy 1:18).

The Turning

A significant role of the Old Covenant prophets was to turn the people back to the Covenant, encouraging them to keep their part. Many did not understand the vital importance of covenant, so the role of the prophet was to be God's voice of explanation, declaration, and proclamation.

The victorious battles of Israel were fought with a greater wisdom of strategy and tactics for winning than we dare employ today. We can define these two vital elements of warfare as strategy and tactics.

Strategy is the science of planning and directing large-scale military operations - specifically of maneuvering forces into the most advantageous position before actual engagement with the enemy. Spiritually, this is done through what we know God has promised us in Scripture. Also, God's strategies are given through our covenant with Him. The true believer must know, understand, and live in our covenant with God.

Tactics are the science of arranging and maneuvering military and naval forces into action or before the enemy concerning short-range objectives. Spiritually, tactics are often revealed to us through the prophetic words we receive which can include dreams and visions. Through these revelatory gifts, we are given precise arrangements

CHAPTER 5 - CONTENDING FOR VICTORY

and maneuvers to fight and win the battles along with the strategies gained through covenant and Scripture.

Prophets were often sought by Israel's kings because they heard the voice of God for going into battle and winning it. They were gifted to hear God more clearly than those who did not want to hear His voice. Warfare for Israel was simply won using God's strategy and tactics. Today we find this tough because we are deficient in trust toward God. Our coming short in believing Him will come to maturity through our intimate, loving relationship with our God. Loving and obeying God builds confidence in the Christian to believe that we are indeed hearing Him concerning the strategies and tactics of spiritual warfare. When God commanded the people to engage in battle, He was their forward observer and commander of the elite forces of the heavenly realm. He promised He would go before them and when Israel's kings heard, responded, and obeyed the strategies of God, victory occurred. Israel's strategies came to them through the promises written in the Scriptures. They received hope and assurance through the trusted prophetic word of the Lord which contained the tactics to follow God's plan for victory.

In modern warfare, we are trained to fight in an arena of our given strengths. A soldier today is equipped to go into battle with the heart and mind to win because of the strategic training he receives. He must be fully and completely ready, knowing the chain of command so as not to break ranks during battle. Modern soldiers are trained as a team of warriors to fight offensively and defensively. They know their weapons; when and how to use them to take, capture, and keep the stronghold. Knowing and practicing such techniques comes through those practiced in the history of winning and the knowledge of new weaponry and ways of warfare. We must apply these principles to the spiritual battles in our lives. Winning requires training of the most elite combat force on earth who willingly receives orders, strategies, and tactics from our Heavenly Commander.

In the New Covenant, God turns the hearts of His people through speaking to their potential. Knowing one's potential is why edification, exhortation, and comfort are premiere in the heart of the writers of New Covenant Scripture. Paul knew and experienced this when he was knocked off his horse with the revelation of Christ. He did not know what happened, but exclaimed, "Who are You, Lord?" (see Acts 22:8).

Prophetic Merit of Victories

The merit of prophecy in winning small and large victories is often lost in our devaluation of the gift. Simple victories are won in the hearts of God's people through being encouraged, built up, and given declarations of well-being. Many precious saints hear God's voice, but when confirmation comes through a prophetic word, victory is won in the soul. These simple victories cause the recipients to rise with courage and move forward in their Kingdom purpose. They suddenly feel and know their connection with Jesus, the Creator of all things. The church today needs significant victories to lead us into taking back the ground the enemy has stolen from us. It is impossible to take the enemy's ground if he has ground in us. Our realizing this is key in building the ultimate combat warrior—the One who dwells in us. If there are areas of doubt, fear, and fleshly lust we cannot battle in the fullness of our call because we have allowed the enemy a legal right to have a place in our soul. If the enemy has ground in our soul (intellect, will, and emotions), the Holy Spirit alerts us to those issues that must be dealt with and replaced with the power and presence of God's nature and love. This battleground must first be won before we can live in the reality of *"He who is in you is greater than he who is in the world"* (1 John 4:4). Until we are free from the enemy's ground in us, we will stumble in our victory as a true overcomer.

When a ministry seeks God to move forward, the enemy often has a predetermined scheme to stop all forward motion. I want to note here that the enemy has no new schemes. He still comes to steal, kill, and destroy God's work in us and through us. His greatest

Chapter 5 - Contending for Victory

weapon is to deceive even the elect *if possible* (see Matthew 24:21-25). God trusts His prophets, revealing to them the schemes of the enemy in an area or local body with whom the prophet connects by ongoing relationship. Prophetic ministry is valued here because of its relationship built on God and His trust in the proper use of the prophet's gift. God is the prophet's priority in friendship, fellowship, and intimacy. In this Covenant, prophets are to bring the knowledge of that lifestyle to all believers. It is through practicing this daily lifestyle that we become engaged with knowing His voice. Remember young Samuel who early on recognized only Eli's voice, thus being unable to recognize God's voice? Young Samuel had not been instructed to know the difference between God's voice and man's voice. Knowing the difference is vital to prophetic equipping in the church today. When Samuel learned to listen to God's voice, that became his focus and passion in life (see 1 Samuel 3:1-10). There was a commitment to be what God was calling him to be! Prophetic ministers are dedicated to the Lord's will and purpose.

In addition to being an equipping ministry, the New Covenant prophet must build a relationship with leaders that God gives them in particular geographic areas. Through trust in the relationship with the leaders and members of local and regional bodies, the prophetic minister works with the teams in providing new direction and revelation where things may have been dull and stagnant. The ministry assigned to the prophet may have some strategies to move forward with God's plan, but will lack in tactics to engage in and win the battle. Knowing these two areas in spiritual warfare is vital for victory. The prophetic word will stir and reveal local bodies with fresh new vision or confirmation to move toward a God-given goal. That goal should include the prophetic wisdom of understanding the interpretation and application of prophetic direction given to these leaders by the engaged prophet.

The prophet will bring warnings to those leaders with whom he has a trusting and ongoing relationship. Often these warnings are of imminent danger revealed through knowing the enemy's schemes.

A Paradigm Shift of Prophetic Revelation

The prophetic minister will have access through his relationship with the Godhead, who trusts him and will reveal to him the plans of the enemy. This level of prophetic wisdom will only be given to those called, nurtured, and seasoned in deep intimacy with the Father, who stand as sons of the prophets. God will release to them the necessary strategies and tactics to win the battle of moving forward in the Kingdom of God.

The Battles of Israel

The historical and biblical battles of Israel will help us see the importance in the relationship of the prophet and leaders of Israel. King Asa was the son of Abijah, a king of Judah. It is written of Asa that he did what was good and right in the eyes of the Lord. Asa removed the altars and wooden images of foreign gods and the high places and sacred pillars were broken down. He in his kingly authority commanded Judah to seek the Lord God of their fathers and to observe the law and commandments. These things were good and right in the eyes of the Lord. Doing the above concerned the known strategy of the law and commandments, which Asa obeyed according to the word of the Lord. God honored Asa and Judah for their obedience to His Word in the Law of Moses. At that time, Judah and Israel were at odds because Israel was serving the false gods of Baal.

Then the Spirit of God came upon Azariah, the son of Obed, and he prophesied to Asa saying:

> *The Lord is with you while you are with Him. If you seek Him, He will be found by you; but if you forsake Him, He will forsake you. For a long time Israel has been without a teaching priest and without law; but when in their trouble they turned to the Lord God of Israel, and sought Him, He was found by them. And in those times there was no peace to*

the one who went out, nor to the one who came in, but great turmoil was on all the inhabitants of the lands. So nation was destroyed by nation and city by city, for God troubles them with every adversary. But you (Asa) be strong and do not let your hands be weak, for your work shall be rewarded (2 Chronicles 15:2-7 emphasis added).

Now when King Asa heard the words of the prophet (the tactics of warfare) he immediately removed all the abominable idols from the land of Judah and Benjamin and from the cities which he had taken in the mountains of Ephraim (Israel) and he restored the altar of the Lord that was before the vestibule of the Lord (see 2 Chronicles 15:8 emphasis added).

A short time later, a treaty was made with Ephraim, Manasseh, and Simeon, and they entered a covenant to seek the Lord God of their fathers with all their heart and with all their soul.

Here we see a spiritual battle won by the house of Judah over the house of Israel who were at odds with each other because of the breaking of God's covenant. Through the strategy of the known written word and the tactical prophetic word of Azariah, a part of the two houses of Israel came back into covenant with God. The prophetic word provides the tactics while the written word often contains the strategy given by God.

King Jehoshaphat's Battle

When King Jehoshaphat became aware of his enemies' plans to come against him, fear came upon him, and he sought the Lord. Because of his position as king, he proclaimed a fast throughout all of Judah. So, they came together and inquired of the Lord. Fasting was a part of God's strategy that they understood as necessary to hear from Him. They came together with one mind and purpose to fast, pray, and declare the name and power of their God. In those declarations, they made an agreement with God's Word to them for protection and safety.

In the midst of the fasting, prayer, and declarations of the people, the Spirit of the Lord came upon Jahaziel the prophet, and he proclaimed the word of the Lord to the people, *"Do not be afraid nor dismayed because of this great multitude, for the battle is not yours, but God's"* (2 Chronicles 20:15b). Then he gave specific tactics for battle position and knowledge of the enemy's location leading to victory in battle based on the word of the Lord. Finally, in obedience to the word and taking that position, Jehoshaphat declared, *"Hear me O Judah and you inhabitants of Jerusalem: Believe in the Lord your God and you shall be established; believe His prophets, and you shall prosper"* (2 Chronicles 20:20b).

Illustrated for us in Scripture, we find the strategy for battle by the King knowing God and His Word. That knowledge rallied the people into finding the plan for battle against their enemies. The strategy was fasting, praying, and declaring the written and known word about God's protection over them. They agreed with what was written and spoken by God.

The tactics for that battle, defining position and action by obedience to the word of the Lord, came by the Spirit to the prophet Jahaziel. Another part of the tactics was the singers and worshippers going before the army and praising the beauty of His holiness. Their words were, *"Praise the Lord, for His mercy endures forever"* (see 2 Chronicles 20:21). Their battle dress in the Spirit was putting on the garments of praise to the Lord. The result in doing this was, *"Now when they began to sing and to praise, the Lord set ambushes against the people of Ammon, Moab, and Mount Seir, who had come against Judah and they were defeated"* (2 Chronicles 20:22).

Chapter 5 - Contending for Victory

Elisha's Word and Jeroram's Assumption

When King Ahab died, the king of Moab rebelled against the king of Israel. Israel's king, Jehoram, then sent a message to King Jehoshaphat of Judah, saying, *"the king of Moab has rebelled against me. Would you come and fight against the Moabites with me?"* (2 Kings 3:7). Jehoshaphat agreed to fight in alliance with the king of Israel. They both assumed that because they were of Israel's 12 tribes that God's will was that they fight together against Israel's enemies, the Moabites. Along with the king of Edom, these three believed they would be defeated by the powerful Moabites. Then Jehoshaphat asked, *"Is there no prophet of the Lord here that we may inquire of him?"* (vs. 11). Jehoshaphat knew that a true prophet would have God's tactical word to win against the powerful Moabites. Then a servant of the king of Israel told them of Elisha the prophet. Elisha, hearing the request, wanted nothing to do with the king of Israel because of Ahab's past sins against God, for Jehoram continued in the sin of his fathers. Had it not been for Elisha's relationship and respect to the king of Judah, he would have disregarded their request to inquire of the Lord.

Elisha then asked for a musician and as the musician played, the hand of the Lord came upon Elisha the prophet. The word of the Lord came to Elisha, saying:

> *Make this valley full of ditches. For thus says the Lord: you shall not see wind, nor shall you see rain; yet that valley shall be filled with water, so that your cattle and animals may drink. And this is a simple matter for the Lord; He will also deliver the Moabites into your hand (2 Kings 3:16-18).*

The next morning the ditches were filled with water and, when the sun arose, the water appeared like blood. Then the Moabites assumed that the kings (Jehoram and Jehoshaphat) had gone to war and killed one another. The Moabites proceeded to the camp of Israel and Israel rose up against them, killing them and destroying their cities. The battle was won, just as Elisha had heard from the Lord.

A Paradigm Shift of Prophetic Revelation

Warring Against Jezebel, Witchcraft, and the Religious Spirit

It is evident our enemy, Satan, does not want to see the Church grow or have positive forward motion further establishing God's Kingdom here on the earth. If we have any wisdom, it is because Jesus is the wisdom of God in us. *"But of Him you are in Christ Jesus, who became for us wisdom from God – and righteousness and sanctification and redemption - that as it is written he who glories, let him glory in the Lord"* (1 Corinthians 1:30-31). In that wisdom, we must recognize that our enemy has no new ways of attack, torment, or deception. We know from Scripture that he is cunning and often uses the same strategy with a change in tactics. That is why we must tap into the wisdom of Jesus. He is the Word of God alive (living and having His life in us). As I have said before I will repeat—we cannot prophesy the Word of God if we do not know the God of the Word. They are one in the same.

Some of our churches have allowed false teachers and prophets to stealth their way into meetings because they sorely lack and trust in the gift of discerning of spirits. Another reason this happens is because of lack of knowledge of God and His Word. Herein, these two areas cannot be remedied without the aid of apostles, prophets, and teachers. We cannot have forward progress in the Kingdom of God when it is secretly invaded by controlling and manipulating spirits. I hear and read such reports often through prophetic and apostolic ministries called to alert the Body of these things. We must remember what Jesus said, *"For false christs and false prophets will rise and show great signs and wonders to deceive, if possible, even the elect"* (Matthew 24:24). I see a current movement that could, in fact, deceive the elect. There is a movement of those seeking after signs, wonders, and miracles more than after their relationship with the Living God. They are consumed with knowing and having the power so as to use it for their benefit rather than the glory of the one true God—the source of real power. I fear for them that they could open a

Chapter 5 - Contending for Victory

door of deception and be gathered into a false movement glorifying a man or ministry. I too often hear more about the man of power than the Lord Jesus, who does the works through us to glorify the Father.

We live in such a time that we must know the desire of God as His elect—not being deceived because we know Him, His voice, nature, character, and likeness. When living fully in His life, it is not possible to be deceived. We must continue to seek out those faithful and trustworthy apostles, prophets, and teachers who demonstrate the love, life, and power of God, consistently pointing the Body toward Kingdom dynamics and intimate, fruitful lifestyles of glorifying the living Christ who always honors the Father.

Apostles, prophets, and teachers lead us toward the best gifts with a more excellent way (see 1 Corinthians 12:28-31). That is the way of God's love, which is the source of all godly power that manifests life, not death.

The more excellent way of love demonstrated by the ministry gifts mentioned above is the only way to overcome controlling and manipulating spirits. Those spirits can only creep into the Body where there is a legal right for them to do so. Pastors and leaders must have godly counsel, ongoing intercession, and those joined with them who are full of God's wisdom. I believe we are coming into the time where we must truly know all those who labor among us. The apostle Paul wrote to the churches concerning the godly qualifications of those called to serve and minister in the church. We must get back to those measures without being religious about it, but rather truly knowing them by the Spirit.

Someone once commented that where there is no control there is liberty. When control of people, ministries, spiritual gifts, and doctrines enter a community of believers, several things might have occurred. Somehow a door in the spirit or soulish realm was opened. Otherwise, control would have no place in the Lord's Body. Consider the Scripture: *"Now the Lord is the Spirit and where the Spirit of the Lord is there is liberty"* (2 Corinthians 3:17). Just before this, Paul

A Paradigm Shift of Prophetic Revelation

is talking about the minds of Israel being blinded and that there remains a veil over them to this day. Since the destruction of the Temple, rabbis had taken over the office of the priests. The rabbis began to make their set of laws to keep the commandments of God. Herein entered the control of the people. Condemnation set in and right worship was lost, being replaced by legalistic rules, which had dire consequences and no hope. Enter the religious spirit of man.

Another area of control and manipulation we first see illustrated is in the time of Elijah the prophet. 1 Kings 16:32-33 states, *"Then he set up an altar for Baal in the temple of Baal, which he had built in Samaria. And Ahab made a wooden image. Ahab did more to provoke the Lord God of Israel to anger than all the kings of Israel before him."* Here is a king of Israel who blatantly disobeyed the God of Abraham, Isaac, and Jacob. Not only that, but he married a Baal worshipper named Jezebel. Baal worship controlled her and was a false god to the Hebrew people.

Of course, most people know that the term "Jezebel spirit" comes from the nature and actions of this wicked queen who continuously controlled and manipulated King Ahab. She forced the kingdom decisions for him by seducing his thoughts and actions to her desires. What true king of Israel would build a temple and a wooden image to a false god?

Following are some characteristics of Jezebel and the spirit by which she lived. She was rebellious against Israel's God, YHVH; against the authority of her husband; she was manipulative; and she took control over her husband's areas of power. If we break down her name in Hebrew, we get *one who lives without cohabitation*. By marrying King Ahab, she was able to manipulate her way into the prime leadership of Israel. She killed many of the prophets who were God's spokespersons to Israel and Judah. The prophets were her worst fears and enemies because they spoke and stood for the commandments and covenants of God to His people.

The spirit of Jezebel desires to dominate the will and emotions of others, especially leaders. These are just some of the ways in which

Chapter 5 - Contending for Victory

this spirit controls leaders, worshippers, and the immature and weak people in today's church.

We combat the Jezebel spirit through first recognizing the spirit operating through a person's life. We must acknowledge that they may or may not realize they and their actions are being controlled by this spirit. Our war is not against the person, but the spirit of Jezebel using them. The first order of combat is prayer and intercession for the individual to recognize the circumstances of why they are living in rebellion against authority in the church. I believe this applies to all spirits addressed in this section.

We must remember that our weapons are not of the flesh or our soul but in our thoughts or ideas about what we should do in combating the enemy. The enemy will always attack a weak point in any person or situation. Those attacks are primarily in the defeated areas in the soul of any believer. The full armor of God assumes a victorious position. That is Christ's place and we are *in* Him, and He is *in* us in all the fullness of the Godhead bodily. The weapons of God are mighty through Him and His redeemer Jesus Christ in us, the hope of glory. When we battle these spirits, we must have the mind of Christ, knowing that Christ has the mind and heart of the Father before He takes any action. When we have the mind of Christ, we live in His likeness and Christ-likeness is our final realm of victory. All warfare is done in the fullness of God's love because His power is in His love, His love is in His Son, and His Son is in us.

There are many excellent books written on specifics in our battle against Jezebel, witchcraft, and the religious spirit that will enhance your knowledge in winning this battle.

Prophecy and Spiritual Warfare

When the church enters into spiritual warfare, there are certain things we do as God gives us strategy from the written Word concerning our battles. We know that we are to be strong in the Lord and the power of His might and always have on the full armor of

A Paradigm Shift of Prophetic Revelation

God. The church must also know our enemy's schemes by which he wages warfare against the saints. In Ephesians 6:10-18, we find the purpose and position of each piece of armor designed for face-to-face battles. Along with the sword of the Spirit, which is the Word of God, we must remain steadfast in all prayer and supplication in the Spirit. When we wear the full armor of God, the enemy knows we stand as watchmen with all perseverance and supplication for all the saints. Watchmen watch and pray, just as Jesus commanded the disciples in the Garden of Gethsemane to "watch and pray." Having the full armor of God is a protective and offensive power of position to perceive the coming enemy and his scheme for the time. When we are in that kind of prayer, believing *in* Him is the same as believing *as* Him. He had no unbelief because He knew and saw what the Father was doing at all times. We, the church, must have our correct identity in our Christ-like position with the Godhead. He is the Son, and we are becoming sons conformed to the image of Christ—that is our position and authority. Our authority is not a gift, but grows out of our relationship with the Godhead. True relationships build trust which is the seed of God's love.

We stand strong as warriors through our conduct in the Gospel of Christ, standing fast in one spirit and one mind, striving together for the ultimate victory. In our union of strength, we are not terrified by our adversaries, which to them is a proof of their perdition and to us salvation from God (see Philippians 1:27-28).

When we are in Him, and He is in us, the enemy only sees Him because *"we have died (been buried out of sight) and our lives are **hidden** with Christ in God"* (author's paraphrase Colossians 3:3). Hidden means to escape notice and when He is our life, our old man disappears because we died when He died. When we fail to live that lifestyle, then we have resurrected a part of the old man that lives in fear and torment of the enemy. The old nature is dead to sin and now alive to God in Christ Jesus our Lord (see Romans 6:4-11). We (the old man that died) escape notice because Christ is the fullness of life in the believer. In essence, the battle belongs to the Lord in us and

Chapter 5 - Contending for Victory

through us. Our role in this is not to allow sin to *reign* in our mortal body, for if sin reigns, then we have resurrected a part of the old nature that died to sin. The believer is now through the process of spiritual development—knowing and becoming the truth and able to do the things that Jesus said we would do (see John 14:12-14).

Finally, we have seen one example after another of how the prophetic word enters into tactics in the finale of battle. We must learn to apply both that which we have active knowledge from Scripture as strategy and that which the active prophetic word provides in tactics.

Paul wrote to Timothy first explaining the purpose of the Law (actually Torah or teaching of Moses). Essentially, Paul is saying that the Law is good if one uses it lawfully, and further that the Torah is not for the righteous person—that is those who have entered into the Kingdom through the sacrificial Cross of Christ. Those that have entered in through the Cross are made the righteousness of God in Christ Jesus (see 1 Corinthians 5:17-21). Again, this is verified by the apostle John who writes in 1 John 3:7, *"Little children, let no one deceive you. He who practices righteousness is righteous, just as He is righteous."* But the Torah (teaching of Moses) is given for the lawless and insubordinate, the ungodly, sinners, those profane and unholy, murderers, fornicators, sodomites, kidnappers, liars, perjurers and anything contrary to sound biblical doctrine (see 1 Timothy 1:9-11). This portion of Scripture is written for us to be able to determine the written strategy for spiritual warfare.

Additionally, Paul writes to Timothy instructing him how to wage spiritual warfare. He writes, saying:

> *This charge I give to you, my son Timothy, according to the **prophecies** previously made concerning you, that **by them you may wage the good warfare**, having faith and a good conscience, which some having rejected, concerning the faith have suffered shipwreck"* (1 Timothy 1:18-19, **emphasis mine**).

A Paradigm Shift of Prophetic Revelation

Examining this word to Timothy, we find this to be not just a statement, but a charge. A charge is a command based on a truth given by God. This charge is about previously spoken prophecies and that through the content of those prophecies Timothy would be given tactics to wage and win the battles set before him.

So again, we see the strategies given through the written Word and the tactics by the prophetic word. I am reminded that we must consider both before actually engaging in spiritual warfare.

Thus, in contending for victory in our spiritual warfare, we must use the fullness of God's wisdom in both the written and spoken words we receive. Engaging the enemy this way gives us not only more knowledge in battle but also the wisdom to win as we allow His life in us to pour out from us, thereby overcoming the enemy of our souls.

Prayer

Father, we thank You for teaching us to war in the wisdom of Your love, strategy, and tactics. Continually remind us through our conversation with You that we wrestle not against flesh and blood, but against principalities, against powers, against the rulers of the darkness of this age, and against the spiritual host in the heavenly places. Thank You, Father, that we first inquire of You before engaging in any spiritual warfare. We do only those things that You lead us and guide us to in the ways of victory over all things that determine to exalt themselves above You.

Amen

Chapter 6

The Revelatory Gifts of the Spirit

Now concerning spiritual gifts, brothers, I do not want you to be ignorant (1 Corinthians 12:1).

In the early years of prophetic experiences, we sometimes had no idea about the *gifts* of the Holy Spirit and their use. The churches I attended referred to *the gifts* as something that happened only in the early church and that they were not for the church in our day because we now have the Scriptures. According to some pastors and leaders, these spiritual gifts had ceased, and God was doing other things only per the Scriptures as they related to modern times.

For me, being "born again" was the beginning of the greatest adventure. The impact of this new life in Christ stirred in me a desire to pray to become *like* Him (Jesus). Although leaders and peers told me that this was not possible, I immediately rejected the thought that one could not attain the likeness of Christ—something I so desperately desired to have. Something profound had happened in my inner man that changed the way I thought and perceived everything in the world.

As I began to grow in the Christian faith, I developed a hunger for God and the written Word. My daily prayer was something like this: "Lord make me more like Jesus today,"—a very effective prayer when prayed with a sincere heart. As I daily prayed that prayer, my hunger and thirst for God-likeness continually increased. I was hooked on being like Jesus. I wanted all of Him that was available to

A Paradigm Shift of Prophetic Revelation

one who believed and followed His ways. I did grow spiritually and intellectually but it seemed as I read and studied the Scriptures more, I was reading about healing, prophesying, and miracles that the church leaders said were "not for today." Because of my prayer and desire to be like Jesus, someone told me about an additional baptism in the Holy Spirit. I had been reading and studying the Holy Spirit and realized that the Bible talked about this baptism. So, in addition to my regular prayers, I began to ask for this baptism and the power of God which went along with it.

When we pray the will of God, we get what we pray for, and shortly after that prayer I received the baptism in the Holy Spirit. This fresh new baptism changed my whole lifestyle once again. Suddenly, I felt a surge of inward power I could not describe. In addition to speaking and praying in tongues, the gift of prophecy which the Holy Spirit had given me as a child began to manifest again. I started dreaming God dreams and having visions and thoughts that could only have come from Him. In reality, I was experiencing fresh things about revelatory spiritual gifts. I knew they were real because of the changes taking place in my spirit and intellect.

Discovering Revelatory Gifts

Finding the roots of revelatory gifts in the breakdown of the nine gifts of the Holy Spirit caused a shift in my thinking and how I prophesied and perceived prophecy. That was the beginning of a new prophetic lifestyle from which I now see the vital importance of those gifts that are revelatory in nature. Why not just sum them up as spiritual gifts? As previously mentioned, in the Greek text there is no word for *gifts* but rather a word is translated as *things or manifestations of the person and power of the Holy Spirit* (my interpretation) come to live (have God's life) in the believer. As I have grown in these gifts and my calling, the wisdom of God has grown within me also.

Rather than refer to the prophetic gift, ministry, or function of a prophet, we tend to focus on the gift of prophecy, the ministry, and

CHAPTER 6 - THE REVELATORY GIFTS OF THE SPIRIT

the function. In doing so, we lose the real meaning of those gifts that are revelatory in nature. This idea confuses some in the Body of Christ that are new to the gifts of the Spirit.

So, what do I mean by revelatory gifts of the Spirit? Simply, they are *spiritual gifts (of the Holy Spirit) that reveal* the heart, mind, and purposes of God often used in conjunction with speaking, writing, or seeing in the prophetic realm. I want to begin with the Scripture in Amos 3:7, *"Surely the Lord God does nothing, unless He **reveals** His secret to His servants the prophets"* (emphasis added). The Hebrew word used here for reveals is *galah*. Used in the context of this Scripture, it has to do with God's laying bare, exposing, revealing, uncovering, and disclosing His secrets to the prophets who are His servants. Taking this into a New Covenant perspective, His prophets today are no longer servants, but also His friends (see John 15:15). Being a friend of God brings us into a deeper, more intimate relationship with the Father as sons. We now communicate with the Father in the same way that Jesus related to Him—doing and saying only that which He teaches, speaks, or shows us. Jesus was the example of how we are to connect with the Godhead just as He did with the Father while in the form of a man. This new relationship of the prophetically gifted now has the responsibility of maintaining oneness with Him in the integrity, nature, and likeness of God. Living this new lifestyle is a part of the process of our spiritual and prophetic growth *"until we all arrive at the unity implied by trusting and knowing the Son of God, at full manhood, at the standard of maturity set by the Messiah's perfection"* (Ephesians 4:13 CJB).

Looking at New Covenant Scriptures, we find reference to prophecy revealing the secret of men's hearts in 1 Corinthians 14:24-25 that states:

> *But if all prophesy, and **an unbeliever or an uninformed person** comes in, he is convinced by all, he is convicted by all. And thus **the secrets of his heart are revealed**; and so, falling down on his face he will worship God and report that God is truly among you"* (Emphasis added).

A Paradigm Shift of Prophetic Revelation

Note something often missed here concerning the persons to whom Paul is referring—*an unbeliever or an uninformed person*. In most services, we tend to aim at those within the learned community or congregation. But prophecy even for the assembled people is more specifically aimed at these two categories—*the unbeliever or the uninformed person* (a new believer). God is concerned in prophecy *first with those two types of people.* We see here a significant change from the Old Covenant prophets to that of a New Covenant prophecy in the Church. The Old Covenant prophets had a message of repentance to God's people Israel—repentance to return to the covenant God had made with them specifically. In the New Covenant, there is still a need for repentance and that is expressly toward our sin in resurrecting the old man (the fallen Adamic nature), which Jesus' work on the Cross redeemed, making us into the new creation man (see 2 Corinthians 5:17-21).

We must practice our relationship of love with the Godhead more than our love for the gift of prophecy. Several things are addressed here by the apostle Paul. Prophecy, when given in a meeting (or for that matter anywhere), will touch unbelievers or the unlearned person's heart. As our love relationship with God increases, the power and purity of the prophetic come forth as spirit and life (see John 6:63). That is the Spirit and life of God as He has it in the absolute sense. The power of the prophetic word coming from the spirit of the sincere prophetic believer contains God's intent for the recipient, therefore revealing the secrets of their heart. Hearing this causes them to humble themselves and worship God, reporting to others that God is among that group or an individual speaking prophetically. The Greek word *revealed* in the Scripture above is *phanerous* meaning conspicuous, apparent, manifest, visible, evident, plain, clear, or open to sight. Only the Spirit and life of God in the prophetic speaker can reveal such things. The process of the prophetic word opens a window or thought in the spirit of the speaker giving them insight into God's heart and intent for the recipient of the word. When spoken, it has the power to affect the

Chapter 6 - The Revelatory Gifts of the Spirit

heart and mind of the one receiving. Therefore, we can refer to the gift of prophecy as a revelatory gift of the Holy Spirit.

Defining Revelatory Gifts

I believe the following gifts of the Spirit are also revelatory in nature and want to discuss and identify their use in the flow of prophecy. The gift of a word of knowledge, the gift of a word of wisdom, and the gift of discerning of spirits all reveal something in the spiritual realm of God and are an adjunct to prophetic speaking, seeing, and hearing. I list them and their meanings below:

The gift of a word of knowledge is a specific piece of divine information revealed by the Spirit about a person, place, or thing that is either past, present, or future. It is used as the revelation—information given to the prophetic speaker, writer, or singer. In the anatomy of the prophetic word (see pg 123), this divine information (word of knowledge) will require an interpretation that must come from the Spirit of God from whom the information was received. We must never make up our interpretation via our thoughts or knowledge, but must pause and ask God for the interpretation of the revealed information.

The gift of a word of wisdom is divine insight into the plans, purposes, and intents of God for a person, place, or thing. It is a part of the prophetic word as wise and godly attitude directing the ability to judge rightly following the soundest course of action in the recipient's life. In the anatomy of a prophetic word, the *word of wisdom* can be considered *the application* of the information (word of knowledge) and a part of the interpretation given the prophetic speaker or writer.

The gift of discerning of spirits is supernatural revelation given by the Holy Spirit to see, know or distinguish what's in the realm of the spirit. Therein, we will intuitively know what is and what is not of God's Spirit, angelic spirits (good and evil), human, or evil spirits. (For more details of this gift, see the author's book: *The Face of Prophecy: Determining the Truth*).

A Paradigm Shift of Prophetic Revelation

These three revelatory gifts are spiritual tools in the prophetic speaking process given to the prophet by God, bringing His clarity to the prophetic speaker when releasing a word in prophetic flow. To help us understand better the particular use of these gifts to those beginning in or those experienced in prophetic speaking, let's look at some of the ways in which God speaks to us through these revelatory gifts.

The gift of prophecy is the oral (spoken) or written words inspired by the Holy Spirit that combine the anatomy of revelation, interpretation, and application, then communicating prophetically to the recipient in the love of God.

Prophecy is man speaking forth God's heart, mind, and purpose by inspiration of the Holy Spirit. Speaking forth like this incorporates the revelatory and prophetic things of the Spirit resident in the one speaking. Prophecy primarily builds up, encourages, and communicates a fuller counsel of God to His people.

God releases information to the prophetic speaker via:

A Word of Knowledge. God speaks Spirit to spirit. God is Spirit. Our spirit is that part of our being God created in the image of the Godhead—Father, Son, and Holy Spirit (see Genesis 1:26-27). The spirit of man is either a part of the nature of fallen man (Adam after the fall) or the nature of God in those who are born again of God's Spirit through the death, burial, and resurrection of Jesus Christ. Those who are born of the Spirit through faith in the process of Jesus' work on the Cross are now reconciled to God by that act of God's love to us. Thus, His Spirit speaks directly to our spirit, and we process that information through our soul and at times our body.

We must remember that we are a three-part being—spirit, soul, and body. God created us that way, and He can use any part of our being to get His message to us. Let me suggest that because He is Spirit that He speaks to our renewed (born again) spirit and we process that message through our soul and body. The soul contains our intellect, will, and emotions. Our body is the physical temple of His Spirit in which He dwells in all the fullness (see Colossians

Chapter 6 - The Revelatory Gifts of the Spirit

2:9-10). *"Do you not know that you are the temple of God and that the Spirit of God dwells in you"* (1 Corinthians 3:16)? And again in 1 Corinthians 6:19 *"Or do you not know that your body is the temple of the Holy Spirit who is in you, whom you have from God and you are not your own?"* I want to add a major thought here that much of the Body of Christ lacks in taking care of this temple. We eat poorly and exercise little, and God created the physical body for proper eating habits and exercise—after all it is a living temple of His Holy Spirit. We must also remember that our soul is in the process of being saved and if we allow unholy thoughts, attitudes, and actions into our soul, we are opening a door to the ungodly realm and our prophecies are affected adversely (see Hebrews 10:39; James 1:21.) We will talk more about this in Chapter 7 - Process of Pure Prophetic Words.

Knowing the above as being truth then, prophets communicate with and through God's Spirit dwelling in them. Nehemiah 9:30b states, *"And testified against them by Your Spirit in Your prophets."* Further Daniel exclaims upon the interpretation of his visions given by God, *"I, Daniel was grieved in my spirit within my body, and the visions of my head troubled me"* (Daniel 7:15). Daniel had received visions from God in his spirit and could not make sense of them through his mind. He had just received visions of the Ancient of Days and saw *"One like the Son of Man coming in the clouds of heaven! He came to the Ancient of Days, and they brought Him near before Him"* (Daniel 7:9-10:13b). Then Daniel had to consult one of those in the vision and asked him the truth of all this. *"So he told me and made known to me the interpretation of these things"* (Daniel 7:16). Just as the revelation (information) comes from the Spirit, so also and perhaps most importantly, the interpretation comes from the same Spirit.

Joseph makes it clear in Genesis 40:8 *"Do not interpretations belong to God?"* Also, Daniel was known as the man in Nebuchadnezzar's kingdom *"in whom is the Spirit of the Holy God"* (Daniel 5:11). When the king's astrologers, magicians, and soothsayers could not interpret his dream, Daniel spoke and said *"But there is a God in heaven who*

A Paradigm Shift of Prophetic Revelation

reveals secrets, and He has made known to King Nebuchadnezzar what will be in the latter days. Your dream and the visions of your head upon your bed were these" (Daniel 2:28). We know that it is God from whom both the revelation and the interpretation come in any prophetic impression, trance, vision, or dream.

I want to share some of the ways God gives us prophetic revelation through a word of knowledge, remembering He speaks first to our spirit man, and we process that divine information through our soul and body.

A key Scripture for knowing His voice is John 10:4-5:

*And when he brings out his own sheep, he goes before them; and the sheep follow him, for **they know his voice**. Yet they will by no means follow a stranger, but will flee from him, for **they do not know the voice of strangers.***

We know His voice because He dwells within us and we practice knowing His voice because it will always agree with His love, character, nature, and the spirit of the Scriptures. The sheep were always within hearing distance of the shepherd. This speaks of a relationship that is essential in our hearing the voice of the Good Shepherd Jesus.

The Ways God Speaks

God speaks by impression—a strong sense or knowing from our spirit and communicated to our soul (mind, intellect and sometimes emotions). Knowing Him like this is one of the most common ways God speaks prophetically. It requires knowing and understanding His voice through daily practice in our relationship with God. For the sake of purity of the word, our souls need continual renewal to God's heart and intents (see Romans 12:2; Ephesians 4:20-24).

We hear God in our spirit man via one or two words or a short phrase that we speak by faith because we know His voice and trust

Chapter 6 - The Revelatory Gifts of the Spirit

Him to give us the remaining part of that word of prophecy. This kind of prophetic speaking may include the revelation, interpretation, and application. Much of the time it may sound like our voice which only means we are one with Him. God's voice lives within as His Spirit has a permanent dwelling place in the believer. The word we hear comes from a depth of our spirit man, not our mind (see Nehemiah 9:30a; Daniel 7:15).

Another way we understand Him is what I call an internal or spiritual vision coming from the Spirit to spirit connection with God and revealed visually in the mind. It's what some folks describe as a picture in their mind. Seeing this way requires interpretation from the same One who gave the revelation (information, picture, or vision)—God the Holy Spirit. Much of the time these spiritually displayed graphics are of something we in the natural do not recognize; therefore, again requiring interpretation to complete the prophetic process.

God can speak through an open vision—as if someone turns on a movie screen (animated) or a still photograph and you see it with the naked eye through the Spirit of God living within you. At times, you become a participant (actually live in it), and walk into it as the Holy Spirit prompts you (see Daniel 8:1-3).

God communicates through a trance—defined from the Greek word (*ekstasis*) as a displacement of the mind, meaning the mind and the Spirit of God become one with your spirit– all being done supernaturally by God's Spirit to you. What one may experience is being aware of your body, but your spirit, intellect, and emotions are in the realm of God's Spirit. Often, we see very vivid, brilliant color, and/or hear sounds, together with feeling outside of our normal consciousness.

God speaks through angelic messengers. God sent angelic messengers to many people in the Bible. They are still with us today, and Scripture says of them, *"And of the angels He says: Who makes His angels spirits and His ministers a flame of fire"* (Hebrews 1:7).

A Paradigm Shift of Prophetic Revelation

Many of today's prophetic people see and often communicate with angels who bring a message from God.

God can communicate through sensations (such as physical pain or discomfort, joy, peace, burning) like Jesus experienced when the woman touched the hem of His garment and He felt power go out from Himself for her healing (see Mark 5:23-30; Luke 6:17-19). Many times, those with a healing gift will receive a word of knowledge through this type of experience from the Holy Spirit either touching our body or defining and speaking out an ailment, thereby identifying the place of needed healing or needed encouragement for the person to whom we are ministering.

God expresses Himself through open or spiritual visions—seeing the likeness of someone you may know in the natural superimposed over the person to whom you prophesy. **Scriptural example:** When Elijah asked Elisha what he could do for him before God took him, Elisha asked for a double portion of ***Elijah's spirit*** to have for himself. The sons of the prophets who were standing by saw this happen. *"Now when the sons of the prophets who were from Jericho saw him, they said, 'The spirit of Elijah rests on Elisha'"* (2 Kings 2:15).

God uses a still small voice like a whisper that we hear internally (remember, God speaks Spirit to spirit). I often hear this as God's voice in my spirit, not in my mind. Jesus' statement in John 10:4-5 reminds me,

> *And when he brings out his own sheep, he goes before them; and the sheep follow him, for* ***they know his voice.*** *Yet they will by no means follow a stranger, but will flee from him, for* ***they do not know the voice of strangers.***

We know His voice because He dwells within us and we practice knowing His voice because it will always agree with His love, character, nature, and the spirit of Scripture. The Holy Spirit in us only speaks what He hears from the Godhead and faithfully delivers that to our inward man, and it always glorifies Jesus, the great Shepherd (see John 16:13-15). Finally, Elijah heard God through a still small voice or whisper, even when he was looking for the dramatically supernatural (see 1 Kings19:8-13).

Anatomy of Prophetic Flow

Everything is made up of various things that we cannot see or understand. Prophecy is much the same. As I practiced prophecy over the years after the Lord entrusted the gift to me, I can honestly say I never fully understood how it worked. Truthfully, as I continue to grow in it, I can say that much is still a mystery. What I do understand is the process of the gift working in the prophetic person. Recapping, God is Spirit, and He speaks to our spirit, which is now conformed to His Own. The two become one (see John 17:20-22). He can talk to us in many of the different ways mentioned above.

Let's say that prophecy has a spiritual and oral anatomy and the makeup of that anatomy is first **revelation** (information received by the prophetic person from God through the Spirit). God speaks to our spirit by His Spirit in us (see Nehemiah 9:30; John 10:27-30; 16:13-15; 17:20-21). Next, we may not know immediately what that information means, so it is our responsibility to seek the **interpretation** of the information we receive. We receive the interpretation from the same source that we received the **revelation**, that being the Godhead. Interpretation does not come from our thoughts or imagination, but from the source who is God the Holy Spirit. Once we have the interpretation, we must ask God if there is an **application** of the revelation and the interpretation of the word to be given. These three spiritual elements are what I call the anatomy of a prophetic word and dissecting them reveals the makeup of the various parts that make them whole. The prophetic word then is complete or full when the revelation, interpretation, and application are given to the recipient. At the time, the prophetic speaker may only get one or two parts of a word, and the recipient must seek God for the complete understanding. An example would be the speaker receives and delivers the revelation and the interpretation. It then becomes the responsibility of the recipient to seek God for the application thus receiving the fullness of the prophetic word.

Another important part of prophecy is the love and character of God released when the word is delivered. The apostle Paul writes,

> *Though I speak with tongues of men and of angels,* ***but have not love,*** *I have become a sounding brass or a clanging cymbal. And though* ***I have the gift of prophecy and understand all mysteries and all knowledge,*** *and though I have all faith, so that I could remove mountains* ***but have not love I am nothing.*** *And though I bestow all my goods to feed the poor, and give my body to be burned,* ***but have not love, it profits me nothing"*** *(1 Corinthians 13:1-3 Emphasis added).*

Additionally, Paul writes to the church at Corinth the following. "But he who prophesies **speaks edification, exhortation, and comfort to men**" (1 Corinthians 14:3). The necessity of God's love and these three virtues of His nature express how He desires to speak to people. I consider these the basic expressions and anatomy of New Covenant prophecy. There are other aspects of prophetic speaking that were also covered in the author's previous book entitled *The Face of Prophecy: Determining the Truth*.

Releasing the Prophetic Word

The thought of being wrong is the greatest fear of speaking in the prophetic realm. Fear is a spirit. 2 Timothy 1:7 states, *"For God has not given us **a spirit of fear**, but of power and of love and of a sound mind"* (emphasis mine). Nearly everyone I know with prophetic gifting had to deal with the fear of being wrong when releasing a prophetic word. What helped the most in my experience was just saying that which I believed God was speaking to me. Although I

Chapter 6 - The Revelatory Gifts of the Spirit

must add here, that was just the beginning of understanding the dynamics of correct prophetic flow. Receiving confirmation from the recipient was most helpful when that would occur. Not everyone you share with will confirm the word, but those who do will help build your confidence in knowing that you heard correctly. Practice, practice, practice is the key to building confidence in knowing God is speaking to us. I was blessed to have been prophetically developed in a place of freedom to engage in my gifting.

Remember what we talked about above concerning the anatomy of a prophetic word as being revelation, interpretation, and application? Interpretation is most often the weakest area that errors can occur.

I believe the reason for this is that we tend to interpret with our thoughts, feelings, or emotions rather than listen to the Lord's interpretation. We tend to be in a hurry rather than to take the second or two to listen for God's interpretation.

The same can be said for the application. We do not need to speak with automatic weapon-like rapidity. It is best to talk in a normal tone and pace of speech. This method is so much easier to deliver, and the recipient can more easily remember when the words are not hurried. Prophecy (in terms of interpretation and application) flows best when our hearts (souls-intellect, will, and emotions) are free from judgments, anger, and personal wounds, which tend to mix and infect the prophetic word within the anatomy described above.

I recommend a learning environment for prophetic speaking where a church is seasoned in the practice of prophecy and offers training and protocol or has a prophetic equipping school. The reason for this is that they are already practicing the process of prophecy and/or growing in prophecy and other gifts of the Holy Spirit. Where the Spirit of the Lord is free to move within the congregational meetings and prayer, there is liberty.

A Paradigm Shift of Prophetic Revelation

Prayer

Father, we thank You for releasing the promise of the Holy Spirit to us. He shed Your love abroad in our hearts so that the things of Your Spirit have their foundation in Your love, the fullness of Your power. We embrace Your love as Your love fully embraces us and the things of Your Spirit, which increase Your revelatory nature into our prophetic nature as Your sons. We take nothing for granted except by Your grace, granting a part of Your DNA in the revelatory things of Your Spirit in us. We love You!

Amen

Chapter 7

Processing Pure Prophetic Words

If I speak with tongues of men and of angels, but I do not have love, I have become sounds of brass or clashing cymbal. Now if I have the gift of prophecy and I would have known all mysteries and all knowledge and if I have faith so as to move mountains, but I do not have love, I am nothing (1 Corinthians 13:1-2).

Several Scriptures have impacted my prophetic lifestyle during my time of practicing and equipping prophetic people. One Scripture passage that comes to mind of such influence leads to aspects of the spirit and soul of the prophetic person. isMatthew 12:33-37,

Either make the tree good, and its fruit good, or else make the tree bad and its fruit bad, for a tree is known by its fruit. Brood of vipers! How can you being evil speak good things? **For out of the abundance of the heart the mouth speaks.** *A good man out of the good treasure of his heart brings forth good things, and an evil man out of the evil treasure brings forth evil things. But I say to you for every idle word men may speak, they will give account of it in the day of judgment. For by your words you will be justified, and by your words you will be condemned. (Emphasis mine)*

This Scripture carries a heavy responsibility for every word we speak. I believe this includes how we speak prophetically. Consider

A Paradigm Shift of Prophetic Revelation

the dynamics and the anatomy of the prophetic word process through our soul (intellect, will, and emotions). God speaks to His prophets by His Spirit in them. Words have power to bless or curse (see Proverbs 18:21). Paul writes *"He who prophesies **speaks to men for edification, exhortation and comfort"*** (1 Corinthians 14:3 emphasis mine). In today's church those who equip us prophetically must have their own spirit entirely engaged in the character and nature of the Godhead. We so often take for granted that once we are saved and baptized in the Holy Spirit that everything is cool. The reality is that our spirit is one with God, but our soul remains to some degree aloof from the new nature. This was very evident to the apostle Paul as he wrote his letters to the Roman church and those at Ephesus about being renewed and being transformed in the spirit of their minds; and about putting on the new man (see Romans 12:1-2; Ephesians 4:17-31). His writing discusses the condition of the soul after the spirit is re-born in the nature and likeness of Christ. Our souls are too often overlooked in every area of the church's ministry and in our new life in the Spirit of God. Paul also prayed for the church at Thessalonica to not render evil for evil, to not despise prophecies, and finally for us to *"present your whole spirit, soul and body preserved blameless at the coming of our Lord Jesus Christ. He who calls you is faithful, who also will do it"* (author's paraphrase, see 1 Thessalonians 5:23-24).

Spirit and Life

Prophetic speaking carries with it an enormous responsibility. Before looking at those responsibilities, let's examine the process of spiritual growth and how that affects the prophetic person's nature, character, and lifestyle. If you call yourself a Christian, every non-believer who acknowledges that is watching you and the kind of life that you portray. It is not just what we say but what we do in the transparency of daily living.

Chapter 7 - Processing Pure Prophetic Words

Spiritual growth is a naturally supernatural process in the life of every believer in Jesus Christ. When one is born again, what part of His nature does that affect? Jesus spoke the following to Nicodemus when he asked about being born again:

> *Most assuredly, I say to you unless one is born of water and the Spirit, he cannot enter the kingdom of God.* **That which is born of the flesh is flesh,** *and* **that which is born of the Spirit is spirit.** *Do not marvel that I said to you, 'You must be born again.' The wind blows where it wishes, and you hear the sound of it, but cannot tell where it comes from and where it goes. So, it is with everyone who is born of the Spirit"* (John 3:5-8, emphasis added).

Understanding this from the Hebraic perspective, water immersion (baptism) would represent a cleansing of the flesh (person). From the spiritual perspective, our spirit when in the state of Adam's fall, is re-born by the action of the work of the Cross and the Holy Spirit's life entering into our spirit. Just as in the beginning when God breathed the breath of life into Adam's body of dirt (not yet living flesh), he became a living soul or being (see Genesis 2:7). Adam was first a living spirit conceived of the Spirit and nature of the Godhead before he sinned in disobedience to God's Word (see Genesis 1:26-27).

Being believers in Christ, our spirit man is re-born of God's Spirit, which is His image because God is Spirit (see Genesis 1:26-27; John 4:24). This truth makes us aware of the need for renewing our minds to the Spirit of God and His written Word. **Jesus or Yeshua** (His Hebrew name), has the distinct meaning of God's **salvation, healing, and deliverance.**

Our souls can be adversely affected because sometimes we carelessly open a door, allowing Satan access through which comes demonic oppression (see Acts 10:38). That access can come from many sources in our time—especially the media, which includes things we see, hear, read, and embrace as truth, but which are not of God's Kingdom. Anything outside of God's will, which is revealed to us in the Scriptures, can affect our soul adversely. Soul in the Hebrew is: ***nepes***; meaning life force, the seat of emotions and desire. In the Greek, soul is defined as ***psuche;*** meaning mind (intellect), will (old nature verses new nature), and emotions (desires, feelings), all a part of the whole created man—spirit, soul and body.

The church today carries the same power and authority to heal those oppressed by the devil, for God is with us and in us. Jesus came to heal the brokenhearted and liberate the captives, characteristics of our being set free from demonic oppression (see Isaiah 61:1; Luke 4:18; Acts 10:38). Once that deliverance takes place, it is vital that the mind, will, and emotions are renewed to God's character, likeness, love, authority, and power. I believe this is a critically overlooked issue in the Body of Christ today. We have allowed world-based counseling into God's spiritual Kingdom. This compromise and others like it have caused us to lose the power and authority of God in many areas of life. Our minds have been confused by incorrect identity and lack in our relationship with God and His Word because we have allowed worldly thought and programs into biblical Church and Kingdom structure.

Because of our use of mundane programs and philosophies, pure ministry and prophecy have been filtered through unsanctified thought and reason. This mindset must change as we return to God's plan for dealing with the soul and body. Our minds must be renewed to God's ways and not be conformed to the ways of this world. Paul makes this very clear:

> *I beseech you therefore, brethren, by the mercies of God, that you present your bodies a living sacrifice, holy acceptable to God, which is your reasonable service. And do not be conformed to this world but be transformed by the renewing of your mind, that you may prove what is that good and acceptable and perfect will of God (Romans 12:1-2).*

Chapter 7 - Processing Pure Prophetic Words

Why does Paul say submit your bodies a living sacrifice? The human body contains our spirit (born of God's Spirit through the work of the Cross and the temple of the Holy Spirit). The soul, intellect, will, and emotions (heart) are an inward part our body. So, Paul is saying to present your whole being as a living sacrifice (see also 1 Thessalonians 5:23). God is still working in the entire man so that we are complete in Him *"who is the head of all principality and power"* (see Colossians 2:10).

The spiritual aspect of the renewing of one's mind transforms us into another being. The intent here is to be transformed into the character, love, and likeness of Christ in intellect, will, and emotions. The intellect, will, and emotions are the exact place in our being where the prophetic word is processed from our spirit, by that which we receive from God's Spirit. Think of it simply this way, God speaks to our spirit (God is Spirit) and we process that divine information, revelation, or vision through our soul (intellect, will, and emotion). If any part of our soul man is still practicing anything of the fallen nature, the prophetic word can be infected by the old nature not yet dealt with. By "any part of the soul," I mean anger, unforgiveness, secret sin, anything that is not of the fruit of the Spirit that we have not given over to God but hold onto like an idol.

This can produce an impure word regardless of our intentions. Herein is the reason that we must renew or restore our minds after being re-born of God's Spirit. To restore means to return back to the original creation intent of God's man, Adam, before the fall. Jesus and His work on the Cross (death, burial, and resurrection) is the only way to that kind of restoration. He is *"the way, the truth, and the life. No one comes to the Father except through Me"* (see John 14:6). The Holy Spirit is the power source of God living (fully alive) in us and with His help, the soul can be renewed back to the original intent of the creation. *"But the Helper, the Holy Spirit, whom the Father will send in My name, He will teach you all things, and bring to your remembrance all things that I said to you"* (John 14:26). Jesus is the Word of God. He said that *"he who has seen Me, has seen the Father"* (see John 14:9). The Holy Spirit also reveals and glorifies everything that Jesus and the Father are in the Kingdom of God which also dwells in us.

> *However when He, the Spirit of truth, has come, He will guide you into all truth; for He will not speak on His own authority, but whatever He hears He will speak; and He will tell you things to come. He will glorify Me, for He will take of what is Mine and declare it to you. All things that the Father has are Mine. Therefore I said that He will take of Mine and declare it to you"* (John 16:13-15, emphasis added).

Knowing and living these Scriptures are a start in relationally renewing our minds in Christ-likeness. As our relationship with Christ and the Father grows spiritually, so also is our mind renewed through the Helper. We finally come to the place of knowing that, as we speak for or about Him, we move toward Jesus' own word becoming spirit and life in us and through us. That is the goal!

The Process

An intimate relationship requires two persons living a life engaged in the dialogue of love, joy, peace, longsuffering, kindness, goodness, faithfulness, gentleness, and self-control (see Galatians 6:22-23)—all fruit of the Spirit. The fruit that is grown comes from the seed that is sown into the soil of the soul. The fruit of God's Spirit is planted from the seed of Jesus' death, burial, and resurrection. Fruit is produced through the process of growth in fertile soil and the proper atmosphere. The same applies to the renewing of our minds. To build a relationship with God requires fertile spiritual soil and healthy spiritual environment. The fertile soil is God's Spirit living as one with us and in us providing the way to the nature of His Kingdom.

Chapter 7 - Processing Pure Prophetic Words

Love for Him first comes from Him, for He first loved us. We do not know love if we do not have an intimate relationship with Him. To prophesy without love is just making sounds or noise that has no useful Kingdom power to transform our being. When love is planted in fertile soil, it produces more love without the attachment of fear because perfect love—God's mature love—casts out fear because fear has torment (demonic oppression). Demonic oppression comes through an un-renewed mind that is conformed to the god of this world. Worldly doors that are open corrupt the soul to the occupation of the devil.

God's love is the first key to renewing our minds. Loving Him and **knowing that He loves us** is not just a mental or emotional mindset, but rather is fully engaged in pure relational dialogue within the fruit of the Spirit. When we truly engage in this kind of relationship, joy is produced between God and our total being. Joy is the fullness of God's love in us. Jesus said,

> *As the Father has loved Me, I also have loved you; abide in My love. If you keep my commandments, you will abide in My love, just as I have kept My Father's commandments and abide in His love. These things I have spoken to you, that My joy may remain in you, and that your joy may be full (John 15:9-11).*

Abiding or living in this is the key to renewing our minds to God's love. Abiding means to live and remain in the fullness of Him, knowing, thinking, and believing His thoughts, will, and emotions. Then God's joy becomes our joy in the fullness of that love relationship. God's **love** is the **joy** and stability that brings His **peace** to our intellect, will, and emotions. It can be called the eruption of God's love flooding our soul man when the soul dies to itself.

Love is the root of longsuffering, which can endure daily, bear suffering, and never give in. Longsuffering is proof of true apostleship and a characteristic of God's love for enduring patience. The mind is renewed in stable and godly thinking, never giving in to opposition or persecution. **Longsuffering is love prevailed.** Prevailing love can only produce **kindness**. When love prevails in the heart and mind, kindness is its product.

Kindness prevails out of God's love and **goodness** and is the moral quality of God's Spirit in our intellect, will, and emotions. It is the loving heart of God's Spirit that transforms the mind of the heart into the mind of Christ within us. The heart of His love dwelling in our spirit demonstrates the desire characterized by His goodness. Goodness is another one of God's characteristics flowing from His heart into our spirit, transforming our minds to His likeness.

Goodness and all the above fruit of the Spirit are morally intertwined with **faithfulness,** meaning to believe and trust, which is God's warranty that guarantees the fulfillment of the revelation He births in the receptive believer. Faithfulness is received the very moment we make our sure decision that Jesus is Lord and when we confess He was born of God's Spirit in a woman of flesh, suffered death, was buried, and finally resurrected by the power of the Father in Himself. Because He continues to fill us with His faith, the heart of His faithfulness transforms and renews the mind practiced in His heart of love.

Faithfulness that comes from the heart of His love in our spirit man produces **gentleness** and **self-control.** A heart filled and lived with and in God's Spirit of love produces the fruit of the Spirit. This fruit, when practiced through the heart, transforms the mind and plants new forms and formulas of thinking in our minds. Our minds are thus renewed with thoughts and intents born out of the fruit of His Holy Spirit, setting a new standard of conformity to the likeness, love, and mind of Christ.

The Holy Spirit is the Helper who brings to mind the things God says about His sons who are led by the Spirit and live in the Spirit. With the help of the Holy Spirit, our minds are renewed to produce the fruit of the Spirit. Renewed minds exude the love, character, and nature of Jesus. The renewed mind indicates a literal change in the way we form our thoughts. We are no longer easily swayed or conformed to the thoughts and intents of this world, but our thoughts and intentions are changed to God's through the Spirit.

Love Is the Key

A pure ministry is the result of God's love manifested in us and through us. Love is the key that produces all genuine and pure ministry. Paul stated in the Scripture at the beginning of this Chapter:

> *Though I speak with the tongues of men and of angels, but have not love, I have become sounding brass or a clanging cymbal. And though I have the gift of prophecy, and know all mysteries and all knowledge, and though I have all faith, so that I could remove mountains, but have not love, I am nothing (1 Corinthians 13:1-2).*

In essence, a prophetic ministry without God's love comes to two final destinations. Making noise and being nothing, it becomes useless words or expressions that fail to move the heart of man into the realm of God. But prophecy manifested with God's love to any person, place, or created thing will bring change, life, joy, peace, and power to that entity.

Love is the power of God to change the heart and life of humanity through the work of the Cross of Christ. Godly love is absolute life, His life, transferred from the believer to the church and the world.

Years ago, I spent several months praying and asking the Lord "Where is your power in the church today?" On July 4, 1991, I received an answer from the Lord. Part of the answer came like this. "You asked where is My power in the church today? My power is in My love and My love is My Son and My Son is in you." His love is in the believer, manifested through the Holy Spirit who dwells in us. *"Now hope does not disappoint, because the love of God has been poured out in our hearts by the Holy Spirit who was given to us"* (Romans 5:5).

As that became more of a reality to me personally, I began to ask the Helper to teach me how to manifest God's love in my life based on the promises in His Word. I started to love people from His perspective and not my own. In that process, I realized that because God's love dwelled in me, it would be that love that pushed the prophetic word out of my mouth.

God is love. That being true, then all prophecy has its origin in the loving heart of God for all who receive true prophecy. His love produces all the fruit of the Spirit. Prophecy then contains love and all fruit of the Holy Spirit. Prophecy spoken in the power of God's love will cause change that builds, exhorts, and arouses Shalom, true peace, in the heart and atmosphere of those receiving.

Love in prophecy is the key that sets all the captives free from receiving again the bondage of fear, for perfect love casts out fear. Real, loving prophecy will never cause torment; only love, joy, peace, longsuffering, kindness, goodness, faithfulness, gentleness and self-control. The goal of prophecy is the peace of God's power released into the earth through those sons of God in which it found its purpose.

Renewed Prophetic Words

Revisiting the two primary Scriptures of this Chapter, we know the following things (which is more than another Christian principle carved out of context by the church to make a point). We are concerned here with a purer word of prophecy where the whole spirit, soul, and body of the prophetic speaker are concerned. Principles are good, but a lifestyle of the fully renewed man in Christ is the goal. The

Chapter 7 - Processing Pure Prophetic Words

church needs these manifest prophetic sons of God now in the times we live. Deception and corruption are ever-increasing on the earth and have crept their way into parts of the Lord's Body because of unrenewed souls. The apostle Paul saw the problem in the early church and perhaps because we have allowed sugar water in the Word of God, our hearts and minds have been diluted and lack purity.

To restore prophecy and prophets to God's intent for the New Covenant, we must take heed to the whole of Scripture, prayer, worship, and the promises of God for the restoration of all things (see Acts 3:19-21). I believe we are living near the end of that restoration spoken by all the prophets since the world began.

Now is the time for us to know Him and the power of His resurrection in us, and have our minds renewed to His completeness as described above; engaging in the fruit of the Spirit in the whole nature of Christ in us. When we need help with this or any process of Kingdom life change, we can immediately ask God, the Holy Spirit (the Helper), to help us engage with Him in the transition.

As we begin this process now in our equipping prophetic people, we will see and experience actual authority, power, and wisdom in our prophetic speaking and writing. God is birthing these characteristics into His prophets who equip us in these times so that when perilous times suddenly come upon us, we will be prepared to speak God's revelation with accurate interpretation and manifest application to those called and sent forth into the darkness as vessels of His light—saving, healing, and delivering those wavering and lost in the deception of darkness on the earth.

The pure prophetic army of the coming time of darkness will be bearers of His light, arks of the New Covenant, and warriors of a new heaven and a new earth because that which is in their hearts will be on their tongues as the message of God.

A Paradigm Shift of Prophetic Revelation

Prayer

Father, You have spoken Your heart to us, saying "be holy as I Am holy." We as prophetic sons desire to express those things of the Holy Spirit, proclaiming that which is pure, noble, just, lovely, and of edification, exhortation, and comfort. In seeking the holy life of Your Son, we become sons in His likeness and speak forth pure words of prophecy that glorify and exalt you.

Amen

Chapter 8

Led by the Spirit of God

For as many as are led by the Spirit of God, these are the sons of God (Romans 8:14).

Our ultimate goal is to speak prophetically in oneness with God's Son, Jesus. We must also determine true prophecy from the same perspective. We must keep in mind the process of the renewing of our souls—mind, will, and emotions—spoken about in the previous Chapter. Having our mind renewed is a vital part of the process of our prophetic development. All prophecy in the New Covenant declares that *"the testimony of Jesus is the spirit of prophecy"* (Revelation 19:10b). When we come to terms with that reality, our prophetic words will have more love, truth, and effect. I continually stress this in my prophetic schools. My desire is to see every student mature in speaking prophetic words of spirit and life. The words we speak must do more than mean something; they must accomplish something in the recipient's life. It is important that we exhort one another toward our identity in Christ more than our prophetic gift.

If we are to live in His image, we must pursue His life in every area, including speaking and judging of prophecy. Jesus is the visible image of God the Father, and the Body of Christ is the clear image of God the Son. We portray that image in Him speaking through us: *"It is **the Spirit who gives life;** the **flesh profits nothing**. The **words** that **I speak** to you **are spirit and life**"* (John 6:63, emphasis added).

"It is the Spirit who gives life" must be more than head knowledge. True prophecy is not spoken by our knowing something about

someone or something naturally. True prophecy comes by the Spirit and not by the will of men (see 2 Peter 1:19-21.) That being the case, then the prophetic words we speak must have their origin in the Spirit of God moving us to speak what the Spirit is saying, showing us via vision or inspiration of God. The inspiration can come through the various ways we have defined God speaking to us in Chapter 6 of this book. The result should be an effect that changes the heart and mind of the hearer.

Speaking this way is our position as prophetic people today. Jesus ascended to the Father, and we now stand in His place on the earth to do those works that He demonstrated. He is the firstborn among **many** brothers. Because He dwells in us in all the fullness of the Godhead bodily, we also, because we are one with Him, speak spirit and life through our prophesying (see Colossians 2:9-10). Jesus is also the first prophet in the New Covenant and the model of all prophecy from this Covenant. It is in the image of the Son of God that we as God's sons and daughters are to live a prophetic lifestyle. We are called to live in godly sonship like the Son of God in the power of the Holy Spirit (see Romans 8:14.)

The Father sent the Holy Spirit as a sign of our covenant with Him. Until today's prophetic church lives and moves and has it's being in the sonship and likeness of Jesus, we will remain in ignorance of our full purpose. Our entire purpose is to live our lives in Christ as a manifestation of His presence in the earth (see Romans 8:19). Speaking prophetically in His image (spirit and life) is a part of that purpose. Just as we are to equip the saints to hear His voice, we must also equip the saints to judge all words spoken as prophecy. We are living in a time of many voices, and when equipped to know and speak as God's voice, we will release true power and authority in the earth. Prophecy then is a vital part of releasing the power and authority of God in the church and the world.

The Lord gave us two New Covenant promises through the prophet Ezekiel. The first is that He would put His Spirit in us and provide us with a new heart (see Ezekiel 36:26). Secondly, Ezekiel

Chapter 8 - Led by the Spirit of God

speaks of a covenant-keeping people who God, through the Holy Spirit, would cause to walk in His statutes and keep His judgments (see Ezekiel 36:27.) These prophecies are the promise of the Father that Jesus spoke about before His ascension.

The release and infilling of the Holy Spirit gave a new endowment of God's power to the believing man. The voice of God was now heard through man's renewed spirit, and that makes us a prophetic people! This outpouring of the Spirit also gave the endowment of speaking and judging prophecy in a new and more positive way. We must not discard the old ways of judging outlined for us in the Old Covenant but hold them as solid, foundational principles. Nevertheless, God released His Spirit to live in us so that we may also see and judge by the Spirit and the written Word.

The Holy Spirit prompts conformity in us as we take on the image of God's Son, making us manifest sons of God. Christ's image and likeness are the focus of all New Covenant prophecy. It is in Him that we make the transition from the Old Covenant prophetic types into the new. The New Covenant prophets proclaim the Kingdom of God; the Old Covenant prophets proclaimed a coming King and Kingdom. We are His Body of Jew and Gentile, the *one new man* prophetic entity living as His image in the earth.

The Lord spoke the following prophetic mandate to all who believe in Him, *"Most assuredly I say to you, he who believes in Me, the works that I do shall he do also; and greater works than these shall he do, because I go to my Father"* (John 14:12). The prophetic works of Jesus are part of the works that He did. We live in those works when we are equipped with the prophetic gifts of the Spirit (see 1 Corinthians 12:8, 10a). When equipped with the things of the Spirit, we then move toward the standard of maturity set by His perfection. Those standards of prophetic speaking and judging are the manifestation of His life working in us.

The Holy Spirit was first manifested in Jesus, the Son of Man. On the day of Pentecost, God released His Holy Spirit into the community of Hebrew believers and 8-10 years later to the believing

A Paradigm Shift of Prophetic Revelation

Gentiles. All believers became sons of God in the earth. When God released the Holy Spirit, this began the fulfilling of Joel's prophecy concerning the last days. The point here is twofold: First, the Holy Spirit continues to pour out from the Father. This pouring out does not stop but is a continuous flow into each believer as they come into the Kingdom through the work of the Cross! Second, He is permeating all flesh with His Spirit in God's Kingdom. Thus, Joel's prophecy is fulfilled daily (see Joel 2:28-32; Acts 2:16-21).

The Hebrew word **shaphak** best defines the pouring out of God's Spirit, meaning *to spill forth the divine nature, to expend life, and intensively sprawl out*. That spilling forth is the life and nature of God through the Spirit. As He pervades our life, we take on the divine nature of Jesus. In that transformation, we are impregnated with the spiritual cells and genes of the Father. The prophetic *things of the Spirit* are part of that infusion distributed by the Spirit.

Words of God's Intent and Purpose

Keeping in mind that we are now prophesying in Him as part of His Body; we therefore only know in part and prophesy in part. That means that the prophet or team of prophetic ministers may have different parts of a prophecy containing revelation, interpretation, and application. Revelation is simply that which is revealed by God to the prophetic person. It is divine information about a person, place, or thing; the past, present, or future; often released by the Spirit to us as the gift of a word of knowledge. Interpretation is the understanding of what the divine information means, and it flows out of the speaker as the gift of prophecy (a prophetic flow inspired by God's Spirit in the speaker). The application of the prophetic word is the wisdom of God released in how and when the word will have an effect on the recipient's life and is often the spiritual gift of a word of wisdom. Wisdom can be described as knowledge applied. I consider these three elements to be the anatomy of a prophetic word so that in the process of receiving a prophetic word, the recipient may understand all or a part of what God spoke to them. The prophetic word that carries the Spirit and life of God will affect the hearer and draw them closer to God. They come closer to the Lord through prophecy because the word inspires and activates the intent and purposes of God in their lives. It will often confirm things God has previously revealed to them privately in prayer, study of the word, dreams and the still small voice of His Spirit within.

Nevertheless, as a Body (meaning all members), we have the mind of Christ. That is, we hold the thoughts, intents, and purposes of God's heart individually and collectively. Thus, in judging New Covenant prophecy, we weigh, discern, distinguish, and thoroughly separate the precious from the vile without the Old Covenant death penalty mindset. In that separation process, we can determine that which is true or false in the prophecy. By that determination, we hold those things which are good and redemptive in the prophetic word. All true prophecy is redemptive because that is the Father's heart.

In a congregational setting of a local body of believers, judging should be prompted primarily by prophetic ministers or elders. If individual words are given publicly, the recipient should ask for assistance from the leadership in judging it.

In my prophetic schools, we practice judging the corporate prophecies given within the class. Usually, I ask the students for specific things in receiving a corporate word from God. I suggest that they ask for the purpose, strategy, and timing of the word. Is it a word for the present, the future, or both? Learning to judge a prophecy is done by the twelfth week of training in the process of two eight-week courses. I am amazed at the accuracy and integrity of their words, which makes the judging process at that time much easier because of the previous weeks of training. In doing this, we agree with the authority and wisdom that God has set in the church. This type of protocol strengthens those prophetically gifted in knowing what to look for in judging prophecy. From knowing how to judge a prophecy, we integrate through our renewed thinking how to speak more pure words. Through this kind of equipping process,

A Paradigm Shift of Prophetic Revelation

we build a stronger, more efficient prophetic base in our churches.

In 1 Corinthians 14:29-32, Paul gives us the protocol structure: *the prophets speak and other prophetic people weigh and judge what is prophesied. They speak individually one at a time so that all may be instructed, encouraged, and comforted.* Speaking prophetically within these parameters brings peace and order in the congregation. When we use this protocol, all attendees have peace about the spoken word. We cover this in greater detail in Chapter 10 of this book.

Determining Prophetic Truth

A huge misnomer in learning the truth of prophecy today is that we judge it for accuracy alone. Some leaders in the church mistakenly do this without the process of prophetic development of the prophetic student. Accuracy is not the ultimate test of judging prophetic words in today's church. When judging New Covenant prophecy, we are not looking for only the accuracy of the word. We also look for the characteristics of God's nature in the anatomy of that word. The prophetic word should be scripturally sound, that is, in agreement with the theme, love, and nature of the written Word. Also, as mentioned in previous chapters, the character, training, and track record of those prophesying is essential in the judging of a prophecy.

Pure prophecy is given to build up, stimulate hope, and produce peace and well-being of the spiritual house or individual. A pure prophetic word will always encourage spiritual growth in the Lord and His ways and will be seasoned with His love. Prophecy will also exhort the recipient toward a prospective future by leading them toward a renewal of godly conduct in personal, church, and Kingdom activity. Prophecy is a gift that helps move us toward maturity in Christ.

Unfortunately, the tendency of the church to over-judge prophecy for accuracy alone hinders the flow of the Spirit and the growth and effectiveness of those with the gift. One area most damaged in our judging of prophecy has come from an Old Covenant mindset dealing with accuracy and timing. While we should apply these principles to prophecy, it should be only *part* of our judging process. Somehow a mindset has crept into the church that says *if it does not come to pass within our time frame, it is a false prophecy.* Having such a mindset is based on the Scripture in Deuteronomy 18:21-22:

> *And if you say in your heart, how shall we know the word which the Lord has not spoken? – when a prophet speaks in the name of the Lord, if the thing does not happen or come to pass, that is the thing which the Lord has not spoken; the prophet has spoken it presumptuously; you shall not be afraid of him.*

Presumption is the issue dealt with in this Scripture. The Hebrew word used for presumption is **zadon**, from the root word **zuyd**, which means one who is **proud, rebellious, arrogant or rude.** To presume something implies that the person speaks out of false authority as if they have authority, yet no authority is given or to take for granted, accepting as true but lacking proof to the contrary. In the above Scripture, the character of the prophet is the issue more than one of accuracy, which is only a portion of the context of these verses. Accuracy is important, but should be judged along with the character of the prophet. If the prophet's character is not mature in the nature, love, and life of Jesus, then the word can be infected by the prophet's character. As stated elsewhere: "If any part of our soul man is still practicing anything of the fallen nature, the prophetic word can be infected by the old nature not yet dealt with."

Whether the character flaw is pride, rebellion, rudeness, or arrogance, meaning presumption (*zuyd* above), then that is truly an area of the old nature and must be dealt with and replaced by humility, love, and godly integrity. That judging process has much to do with the delivery coming from a person who is immature or unlearned in prophetic speaking. It is vital that we not only understand the equipping process, but that we activate the knowledge of judging prophecy through those called, seasoned, and practicing this ministry. In the equipping process, the character and nature of the Godhead are of most importance and should be included at the beginning of equipping prophetic people. Speaking a pure, accurate word has as much to do with the character of the speaker as the nature of the one judging (see 1 Corinthians 14:29-33; note vs. 32, "*The spirits of the prophets are subject to the prophets.*").

The Old Covenant teaching of Moses reveals a standard of judging set by God. According to Jeremiah, part of the New Covenant was that God the Holy Spirit would write the teachings of Moses on our hearts. That being the case, we cannot deny the importance of the Old Covenant writings. As mentioned earlier, Moses received the revelation from God about true and false prophecy. This principle still stands as part of what is written on the hearts of New Covenant believers. The Law (actually translated as Torah–first five books or the teachings of Moses) of God is what is written on our hearts by the Holy Spirit (see Jeremiah 31:33). As Christians, we are grafted into and are part of the commonwealth of Israel (see Romans 11:17; Ephesians 2:12-15). Deuteronomy 13:1-4 points us directly to the New Covenant heart because through the indwelling Holy Spirit, loving and knowing God is written on our hearts. Knowing and obeying Him, His commandments, statutes, and ordinances are a vital part of the first steps in judging prophecy.

Another point to consider is that the apostle Paul states that the things he wrote about speaking and judging prophecy were the commandments of God (see 1 Corinthians 14:37.) This kind of relationship with God enhances our understanding of Him and helps us see prophetic speaking and judging from God's perspective. The writings and teachings of both covenants apply to the established biblical judging of prophecy.

Now is the time to put unsound doctrine about prophecy to rest. The Lord never intended the church to rely totally on institutions of higher learning for its doctrine. The Father compelled Jesus to choose

12 unlearned men as His apostles and in the three and one-half years that they lived with Him, they were in the school of the Spirit. Being Hebrews, they were taught the Scriptures, *Torah* (teaching of Moses), *Nevi'im* (prophets), and the *K'tuvim* (writings) from childhood by their parents. Later, as disciples, Jesus, their teacher, taught them to live the written and living Word as a lifestyle through the Spirit. The apostle Paul, one of the most learned men in the New Covenant, stated that his own preaching was not in the wisdom of men but in the power of God (see 1 Corinthians 2:2-5). The Holy Spirit was given to be the comforter, helper, and teacher of all believers. God established equipping ministries through the written word and the Holy Spirit to promote spiritual growth (see Ephesians 4:11-16).

One of our greatest assets in speaking and judging prophecy is a solid foundation in the written Word of God, the Bible. Prophetic classes in any school should emphasize being rooted and grounded in the written Word. As today's church moves forward in prophecy, we must return to the standards of the early church, which lived by the Spirit and the Word. Both the written Word and the Spirit are vital and necessary for us to live godly Kingdom lives.

Do Not Quench the Spirit

The apostle Paul gained a vast knowledge of God through his studies as a Pharisee in his early years, but God through the Holy Spirit anointed him to bring wisdom and understanding to the Jews and Gentiles concerning prophecy and gifts of the Spirit. He was inspired to establish guidelines on how to speak and determine the truth of prophecy in the New Covenant in accordance with his knowledge of the Old. He understood both Covenants and God's intent for the new from the perspective of an Orthodox Jew who believed in Messiah Jesus. In the Old Covenant, the Spirit of God was quickly quenched by those who did not engage with or who were not inspired by Him. Kings, priests, and prophets were the primary persons who were called upon to interpret Moses' teachings

A Paradigm Shift of Prophetic Revelation

(God's Word). Not all who were part of Israel had a relationship with the Spirit of God as did her prophets and leaders. Amazingly, the New Covenant gives grace to all who have God's Spirit living in them giving today's believers the power to walk and live in accordance with Him. The promise of the Father is spoken from the Old and brought forth as life in the New.

However, similar to the church in Thessalonica, much of today's church has quenched the Spirit. Paul warned them with straightforward words, *"Do not quench the Spirit, do not despise prophecies.* ***Test all things, hold fast what is good****. Abstain from every form of evil"* (1 Thessalonians 5:19-22, emphasis added.) When we despise prophecy, we quench the Spirit. Failing to test all things quenches the Spirit. Entertaining evil thoughts and ways quenches the Spirit. Quenching the Spirit happens because of a shallow relationship with the Lord, the Spirit, and the Word.

Other warning signs of quenching the Spirit are prideful, disruptive, and boastful attitudes among leaders and members of the Body. Humility in Christ is the key to living our lives in the Spirit. Fortunately, these attitudes are changing as we move into the reality of the restoration of all things spoken by the holy prophets throughout the ages (see Acts 3:20-21). We cannot discard the directives we were given for judging prophecy today. We must, as a Kingdom principle, embrace prophecy and the judging of it in our lives today. We cannot embrace one aspect of prophecy and reject other aspects. Before we can begin the process of judging, we should know God's established protocol for speaking prophetically in various settings.

In judging prophecy, we must embrace the Scriptures in 1 Thessalonians 5 above, and in 1 Corinthians 14:29-32, which states,

> *Let two or three prophets speak, and let the others judge. But if anything is revealed to another who sits by, let the first keep silent. For you can all prophesy one by one, that all may learn and all may be encouraged. And the spirits of the prophets are subject to the prophets.*

In weighing any prophetic word, we test its entire content to determine what is good and relevant to the recipient as directed in 1 Thessalonians 5:20-21 above. It is the edification, exhortation, and comfort in the word of prophecy that enhances our lives and helps us in the process of spiritual growth. Even if all New Covenant prophecy were one hundred percent accurate, there would still be a need to judge it. Why? Because Scripture instructs us and we are taught these principles in our discipleship, character training, and equipping experiences.

That which we have learned from previous writings about the faces of prophecy, the Lord's commandments, motives, and character issues leads to determining the truth of all prophecy. Accuracy comes with proper equipping, preparation, nurturing, mentoring, and practice. We know only in part and prophesy in part. As members of His Body, the hand cannot speak for the eye or the foot for the ear. Nevertheless, as the various parts of the Body speak according to the Head, Jesus, the entire purpose of prophecy is unveiled.

The Need for Diplomacy

Because today's church is in major transition, we must look at the need for diplomacy and conduct in our prophetic meetings. We might also call this "protocol," which will be discussed in Chapter 10 of this book. Protocol can be defined as correct diplomatic behavior. This discipline needs to be set up for the various ways, places, and times that prophecy may be given. We should look at it from personal, local, regional and national levels. The regional and national levels would be served and directed by apostolic and prophetic leaders, with prophecies broadcast using social media.

This organization of protocol can be implemented through the coming together of local church leaders. Currently, there is a group of leaders establishing a prophetic council in the Denver Metro area. They plan to operate in a similar manner as the council at Jerusalem described in Acts Chapter 15. Once this council determines what is to be shared about the prophecy concerned, then individual prophetic ministers can deliver the word to the local body in their particular area of the city or region. Having a prophetic council is a pioneering effort that is needed for the church at large.

When the word is for the corporate Body, the region, the nation, or world, we encourage our people to submit it to the designated leadership for judging. Because they have been through prophetic training, they are comfortable with that process and biblical protocol. Once this word is judged by the designated local, regional, national or international council, it can be submitted to those with a prophetic voice in the related areas.

Prophetic Administration

Knowing how to properly administer prophecy is a valid point for any prophetic school, because it affects the content and delivery of the word. We can define administration as that which is ruling or governmental. This rule is not to be law, but the governing of Church and Kingdom authority designated by God in Scripture. It is the responsibility of the prophetic equipper, student, and speaker to properly administer the delivery of the prophetic word.

One aspect of delivering prophecy is to know our measure of authority in God's Kingdom. First, let me express that our authority is not a gift from the Holy Spirit, or from our experiences only. Authority primarily comes from our relationship to the One in authority. Jesus said this,

> *All authority is given to Me in heaven and on earth. Go therefore and make disciples of all nations, baptizing them in the name of the Father and of the Son and of the Holy Spirit, teaching them to observe all things that I have commanded you; and lo I am with you, even to the end of the age (Matthew 28:18-20).*

Chapter 8 - Led by the Spirit of God

The disciples received this authority because they had personally lived 3 1/2 years with Jesus. The authority that we carry in Jesus comes from our relationship with Him. The relationship we have with Him determines how much authority He can trust us with in any given situation. Further, in a local body, our authority is based on the measure of responsibility we have in the governing body of which we are a part. If we function in the ministry of helps, we have no authority to make decisions beyond the ministry of helps, etc. The body always works together in unity; the same is true for the spiritual house of the Godhead.

As previously stated, authority is given through our relationship with the One in authority (Jesus now in us). A good example of governmental authority is shown in the ministry of Paul and Barnabas in Acts 15. Here we have an apostle and a prophetic minister working together planting, establishing, and strengthening local elders in various churches. When they were confronted by religious leaders about the custom of circumcision being a way of salvation, they determined according to their level of responsibility to go to the apostles and elders in Jerusalem. Through a council of authority in the Kingdom, they decided how to approach and solve the problem. They did not take such an important issue upon themselves, but submitted it to a level of authority beyond their own.

The same principle is applicable in prophetic ministry in the church. Based on scriptural principles and practice, every prophet and prophetic minister should be a part of the local church and accountable to that level of authority. Paul and Barnabas were originally sent out from the church at Antioch (see Acts 13). Though they became itinerant, they had a home base of accountability who loved and prayed for them.

Authority in prophecy or prophetic ministry does not come from the level of revelation we receive. If we receive a seemingly high revelation and are part of a local church, our responsibility is to submit it to the leadership before we blurt it out in a public meeting. Doing it in this manner is in order, even if we are a prophetic minister as part of the local leadership. This kind of responsible practice comes from respecting God's order of Kingdom government. We must be true in how we represent the Lord, His Church, and Kingdom government. We never want to misrepresent God by ministering beyond the level and responsibility of authority set by Him in the Kingdom. It is vital to the efficient working of His Kingdom here on earth.

Love and humility are still the keys to godly prophecy. When these attributes of God are incorporated in the administration of prophecy and are part of the equipping process, we will have taken another step toward maturity in the Kingdom. We must equip the prophetic ministry toward levels of excellence in all aspects of Body and Kingdom ministry. Once this becomes the standard, judging prophecy will become an accepted responsibility, and the Kingdom will advance as a force of God's love and power. Prophetic administration is a preliminary step taken before moving into other aspects of the equipping process.

Sons of God

Our ultimate goal of being led of the Holy Spirit is the primary key to our true identity. Again, I want to stress that God's intent is not for us to be known by our gifts, titles, or professions, but by the Spirit of God in us. The apostle Paul writes to the church at Thessalonica the following:

> *And we urge you, brethren, to recognize those who labor among you, and are over you in the Lord and admonish you, and to esteem them very highly in love for their work's sake. Be at peace among yourselves. Now we exhort you, brethren, warn those who are unruly, comfort the faint-hearted, uphold the weak, be patient with all. See that no one renders evil for evil to anyone but always pursue what is good both for yourselves and for all. Rejoice always, pray without ceasing,*

Chapter 8 - Led by the Spirit of God

in everything give thanks; for this is the will of God in Christ Jesus for you (1 Thessalonians 5:12-18).

So, do we recognize those who labor among us by their gifts, titles, functions, or work? No. We are to know one another by the Spirit. It is our spirit man who has been adopted into the Kingdom through the work of Jesus on the Cross. As we grow and live our lives in Him, we become more like Him. We are to be an express image of His likeness, nature, love, and character. We recognize one another through our Christ-likeness, not our gifts and callings.

The intent of God creating mankind was this: *"Let us make man in our image, according to our likeness"* (Genesis 1:26a). We as followers of Christ know that man fell in the Garden and then needed a Redeemer. Christ, the Father's only begotten Son, entered the earth, was born of a virgin impregnated by the Holy Spirit, and became mankind's Redeemer through the work of the Cross. After the resurrection, we who believed were conformed to the image of Christ *"who is the express image of the Father, and who, upholding all things by the word of His power, purged our sins, sat down at the right hand of the Majesty on high"* (see Hebrews 1:3b, author's paraphrase). In that majestic act of the Godhead, the whole creation was in earnest expectation, eagerly waiting for the manifestation of the sons of God (see Romans 8:19-26).

When we are called to prophesy or function as a prophet or in a role of prophetic ministry, we must first and foremost remember that:

> *For as many as are **led by the Spirit of God, these are the sons of God.** For you did not receive the spirit of bondage again to fear, but you received the Spirit of adoption by whom we cry out, Abba, Father. The Spirit Himself bears witness with our spirit that we are children of God (Romans 8:14-16, emphasis added).*

Based on this Scripture and others pertaining to the manifest sons of God on the earth, we must take heed to **"not receive the spirit of fear again to bondage."** It is vital and necessary that in the training and development process, the spirit of fear be cast out through the perfect love of Christ living in the spirit of the prophetic person (see 1 John 4:17-18).

We must be thankful to God the Holy Spirit for distributing the spiritual gifts to us as He wills, always keeping in mind that these things of God's Spirit are not our identity but rather a function representing and glorifying the works of God in the earth. These beautiful things of God's Spirit are most effective when led by His Spirit rather than by our will. When we as prophetically gifted people are led by the Spirit, our gifts will point to us as sons of the living God that the creation is earnestly expecting and crying out for. To Him be the glory!

Prayer

Father, we desire always to be led by Your Spirit and in that we know we will not be led astray. Our hearts and minds are in submission to only your Holy Spirit and we pray our prophetic lives and words will bring you glory and honor in all things that we speak and all things that we do.

Amen

Chapter 9

Experiencing the Prophetic Realm

I was in the Spirit on the Lord's Day, and I heard behind me a loud voice as of a trumpet, saying "I am the Alpha and the Omega, the First and the Last," and, "What you see write in a book and send it to the seven churches which are in Asia: to Ephesus, to Smyrna, to Pergamos, to Thyatira, to Sardis, to Philadelphia, and to Laodicea." Then I turned to see the voice that spoke with me. And having turned I saw seven golden lampstands (Revelation 1:10-12).

During my childhood, I remember significant times of seeing, sensing, and being frightened by the so-called things that go bump in the night. Not many paid attention to those of us who experienced these bumps except to say, "that's just your imagination." Many years later I realized that I was experiencing things in the spiritual realm. One night, I felt the presence of Jesus and saw a glimpse of His likeness in my room—but who would believe me? So, I suppressed it and said nothing. My experiences in that realm became private because no one I trusted would endorse them as real. In those days, I continued to see, sense, and hear things that were not always good in the spiritual realm. I knew something was definitely there, but I had no understanding of the difference in spirits except the experience at the time.

Experiences in my childhood were that I very much sensed God as being real. Much of this was due to my grandmother reading the Scriptures to me and telling me stories about Jesus. As I look back on those times, I know I was sensing God's presence because He dwelled in my grandmother. When she passed away in my teen years, there was no one to guide me toward the Lord. I followed my peers and walked away from seeking God, yet somehow knew He was still interested in me. I often thought of Him and probably prayed, seeking Him in times of troubled teen and early adult activities.

Born Again

My military years were also years of turmoil and confusion about God, though, even without a relationship, I somehow knew He was real. Upon my release from the armed forces, I moved back to Colorado and spent some time with my parents, who then lived in a duplex next to a family with a young lady my age. We met on the front porch and over time as we got acquainted she started talking about Jesus, church, and Christianity. Next thing I knew, I was attending a Baptist church with her on Sundays and Wednesday evenings. The preaching was convicting me of sin in my life, and I went forward to the altar almost every week, yet no one took the time to explain to me why I was there (strange but true). So, I thought I was born again every time I went forward.

About a year later, we were married by the same pastor who had believed that I knew what was happening to my life. We then moved to Northern Colorado where I started attending college, thinking that was the thing to do for our future. I majored in art but did not fully enjoy the other required courses. While attending a local Baptist church, the pastor asked me to give my testimony about being born again. After hearing my weak and misleading story, he said, "we need to talk." A few days later in his office, he explained to me the born again experience took place only once and then shared with me the truth, and I was born again that very moment. How did I know? Because my heart and mind began to function differently! Things were deeper in my spirit, which in turn changed the thoughts and intents of my heart. I wanted only to be like Jesus! I began to meet

Chapter 9 - Experiencing the Prophetic Realm

regularly with that pastor, and he mentored me for the remainder of the time I spent there. I thank God for His love expressed through that man to me.

A New Life

Several years passed and my spiritual life changed day by day. This new lifestyle affected my open-ended question, "where do I fit in this world and what am I to do in life?" God took me on the journey from being an art major in college to suddenly finding a new career in architecture—a divine appointment that would change things even more.

After taking some courses in architectural design and drafting, I took my first job in the field of architecture. God set me in the perfect place to grow in a two-man office with a mentor who was a graduate of the Frank Lloyd Wright Foundation in Scottsdale, Arizona. I spent the next 27 years in the field of architecture where my creative gifts flowed freely.

It was during this time that the prophetic gift was re-ignited from my earlier years as a Christian. God set me on a new course both in my career and especially my spiritual life—a new direction that was not void of trials and troubles. In those difficult times, my un-renewed soul issues formed scar tissue due to my past emotional wounds and deep hurts. I had no idea where to go or what to do concerning the guilt and shame of those earlier years of my life. I needed deliverance, not just counseling. Deliverance came through a local pastor who later became my mentor in teaching the Word. At the same time, I met his wife who was incredibly prophetic and that started a new relationship with the Lord in prophetic gifting. *(God just sets up divine appointments in His time frame, not ours.)*

My relationship with this pastor and his wife caused a sudden surge of spiritual growth in my life. This new way of life affected much in my personal life as well. I seemed to be going beyond where other friends, relatives, and believers dared to venture.

155

A Paradigm Shift of Prophetic Revelation

Much changes in one's life when the prophetic gift begins to develop. Nearly everyone I knew thought I had gone off the deep end as we were all still involved in traditional Pentecostal, Charismatic, and Evangelical churches.

Growing Pains

The longer I was with my mentors, the more the prophetic gift developed. A small group of spiritually gifted people began to emerge, and our home group became one of pioneering the prophetic, healing, and teaching gifts. We were far from being mature, but in those years, little was known about the process of prophetic development. I began to suffer much in the loss of friends and relatives. Much of the pain I experienced could have been avoided if we had a greater sense of love and maturity in our gifting and spiritual growth at the time.

As a small group of pioneers in the 1960s, we all had similar experiences and entirely different backgrounds. Supernatural things began to happen to us in our meetings and homes. Several of us had angelic visitations, lots of dream activity, and some visions. We were all young in these new manifestations of the Spirit and struggled with the question "is this God, me, or the devil?"

Another personal struggle for me in the prophetic gifting was answering the question: *Am I a prophet or just one prophetically gifted?* Not even my peers or mentor had the exact answer for me then as we were limited in our knowledge of the call, the gift, or ministry in those days. Understanding this new dimension of gifting took a measure of time because of the peculiarity of the gift and the lack of knowledge and experience of prophecy in the church. We continued to pursue a greater understanding of what was happening in our lives.

Chapter 9 - Experiencing the Prophetic Realm

Personal Experiences

I have always had dreams but never associated them with God. Dreams were just some mystical phenomenon that everybody seemed to experience. Then, suddenly, I began to understand that God was getting my attention through dreams. I was able to tie things, people, and places to my dreams and God gave grace to me so that some of what I dreamed happened. This amazed me, but I still had no understanding of the symbolism that occurred in so many other dreams. They just did not make sense. I remember some significant dreams about serpents and my stepping on them, crushing their heads, walking among them, and never being bitten. Later, I understood through Scripture that Jesus told the 70:

> *Behold, I give you authority to trample on serpents and scorpions and over all the power of the enemy, and nothing shall by any means hurt you. Nevertheless do not rejoice in this, that the spirits are subject to you, but rather rejoice that your names are written in heaven (Luke 10:19-20).*

I did not get the full understanding at that time, but began to see that God was, in fact, speaking to me. My next question was: *When God speaks in dreams, why doesn't He just make them clear?* Sometime later, after reading in Numbers 12:6, *"Hear now my words; If there is a prophet among you, I, the Lord, make Myself known to him in a vision; I speak to him in a dream."* Wow! God was speaking to me in dreams! Understanding my dream life was another process that took many more years. Today, I still have dreams. Some are prophetic and some personal. My understanding of dreams and their interpretation has become another part of the prophetic process in my life. There is a process in learning about dreams, their interpretation, and fulfillment. Dreams are a major part of being prophetic and living in that lifestyle.

A Paradigm Shift of Prophetic Revelation

Our group of pioneers continued experiencing more of God's supernatural ways in our meetings and personally as well. I remember one evening when we were in prayer I heard footsteps in the room and felt a presence that was very peaceful. I did not look around, but suddenly I saw a man dressed in a white robe with gold trim and wearing a golden band/crown around his head. Alarmed about what to do with this vision, I asked the Holy Spirit about it. He said I saw Joseph, one of the sons of Jacob, and that I was to receive similar blessings given to him in Scripture. Joseph was a dreamer, and he received a most powerful blessing from his father Jacob in Genesis 49:22-26. I asked myself later, why would God want to bless me with Joseph's blessings? Well, God is not a respecter of persons, and He is very intentional with us in being Kingdom people. His heart is to bless and not curse.

Voices, Visions, and Angels

One of the most common ways we begin to hear God is through what can be called an impression. It is a sense of knowing something deep in our spirit man and it is interpreted through the soul as a thought about something or someone that we did not know before. One definition of *impress* is *a marked effect on the mind or emotions; to arouse interest; to plant firmly in the spirit or fix in the memory*. So how does this work in the prophetic? First, God releases the divine information to our spirit. Our spirit then releases the impression to the mind, will, and emotions. The impression is then processed as God's thoughts through our voice to the recipient.

The voice of God is caught in the spirit of a man—our spirit is one with God's Spirit in the Christian believer. In this first step, remember Jesus' prayer for us:

> *I do not pray for these alone, but also for those who will believe in Me through their word; that they all may be one,*

Chapter 9 - Experiencing the Prophetic Realm

as You, Father are in Me, and I in You; that they also may be one in us, that the world may believe that You sent Me (John 17:20-21).

Thus, we hear in oneness with our "spiritual ears" a sound planted in our spirit as one or more words or a phrase which immediately transfers to the soul realm (intellect, will, and emotions) as a word from God. Often, that is only the beginning of something God wants to speak to a recipient. Our next step takes faith (entirely trusting God) that He is speaking what we first hear—we then speak that out as a flow of words, thoughts, and impressions of which we call a prophetic word by inspiration. Remember the prophetic flow comes from our spirit where God's Spirit resides in us inspiring us to speak. The experience is similar to speaking or praying in tongues.

Another way in which God speaks is like what Elijah heard, ***a still small voice*** (see 1 Kings 19:12-13). The point made in the story of Elijah is we don't always look for God in spectacular manifestations but know that He speaks to us in a still small voice. This voice is also heard deep in the spirit of the prophetic individual and is immediately processed through the soul as mentioned above. In Elijah's situation, his life had just been threatened by Jezebel. This evil, ungodly woman had spewed death out of her mouth to the prophet who had just had a victory over the false prophets of Baal who (fellowshipping with and ruled by her) sat at Jezebel's table. Elijah was terrified and needed a sign from God right then! While hiding in a cave, the word of the Lord came to him saying, *"What are you doing here, Elijah?"* In great despair, Elijah told God how he had done all God had asked of him and now thought that he alone was the last of God's prophets in the land. Because his soul was in fear, his state of mind and heart made it tough to hear God. So, Elijah looked for God in the spectacle of a great wind upon the mountain, an earthquake, and fire, but God was not in them. But after the fire was ***a still small voice*** deep down in the prophet's spirit saying again, *"What are you doing here Elijah?"* It was the still small voice that brought relief and strength to Elijah,

A Paradigm Shift of Prophetic Revelation

knowing that he had heard from God and was now at peace and able to receive further instructions about where he would go as God told him to leave the comfort of the cave. *The still small voice of God* assures the prophetic person of the peace and strength of the Holy Spirit leading us to listen before we act or speak.

I want to point out that not all prophets are seers, but all prophets can see in the spirit as the Holy Spirit inspires them in the visionary realm of God. I often refer to some visions as *a glimpse into the spirit realm* or what most can relate to as a sudden picture in their mind. I like to call this an ***internal spiritual vision***. The question most people ask is: "Is this my imagination?" This question is for me dangerous if we are in fact depending on God to give us true spiritual revelation. There is no imagining in the spiritual realm of God speaking to us. Imagining comes from the soul realm and is a worldly pattern of thought and perception. The human imagination defined is the act or power of forming mental images. The spirit of prophecy is from God who sees all before it happens or has happened and relates it to our spirit in union with His own. We must remember that God speaks to our spirit by His Spirit in us—this has nothing to do with the human imagination! (see Nehemiah 9:30; Daniel 7:15-16; Revelation 1:10-12). So even an ***internal spiritual vision*** that comes through God's Spirit in oneness with our spirit is then seen in the eyes of the mind. It may occur for just one or two seconds, but we see it clearly as from God because we know He is faithful. This kind of vision is very common to many other prophetic people in the Body of Christ, including myself (see Matthew 7:7-11; Luke 11:9-13).

Another type of vision not so common is what I call ***an open vision***. The open vision occurs when the Spirit of God releases the eyes of your spirit to see what He is showing you in the realm of His Spirit. You are often aware of your body, but your spirit is caught up in God's visionary realm. To make it as simple as possible it's like someone turns the TV on but there is no TV and no screen. And you are suddenly experiencing through your own eyes a supernatural image either still or animated and sometimes with sound. We understand that God may only speak to the inner man via His Spirit in us. Open visions are not the norm for most prophetic people. For myself, I have experienced only a handful in my life. Below are a few of them. I will describe them and the gifting by which I believe they were received:

In the 1960's, I had been in personal spiritual warfare and knew little to nothing about what to do in those situations. At first, and for many nights, I saw and experienced demonic entities in my bedroom. Experiencing such things was frightening to me as no one had yet mentored or taught me what to do in these kinds of situations. After many desperate prayers asking God to intervene, I began to have some understanding about this. A short time later, I was awakened by an awe of peace beyond anything I had ever experienced. I was wide awake, eyes open, and saw an angel standing in my room. His head and shoulders were high above the doorway and it appeared as if there was no ceiling in the room. His presence was majestic, and he seemed to fill the room. The angel appeared transparent, yet I clearly saw that he wore a white garment with a blue opened collar and he was filled with light and peace.

As I continued to observe in a state of awe, another thing suddenly happened in the vision/visitation. High above the angel and filling the space where the roof and ceiling would have been, I saw the face and shoulders of Jesus. Emanating from Him were streams and rays of brilliant lights of various colors. His eyes appeared with a laser-like brightness as He looked at me with a smile of great joy on His face. He spoke nothing to me, but there was an assurance of divine love and peace filling the entire space of the vision. I knew He was present and that He loved me deeply.

This vision was my first memorable open vision and revealed to me two gifts in the operation of the Spirit. First, *the seer gift* that is described in Hebrew as *Roeh* or *Chozeh,* meaning a beholder in vision or one who sees via prophetic vision. Secondly, *the gift of discerning of spirits* was demonstrated to me as God had granted me to see beyond my natural ability as to what is in the spiritual realm. A

A Paradigm Shift of Prophetic Revelation

short time later, I was in prayer asking the Lord what this meant and why He allowed me to see Him and the angel in a vision/visitation. I heard Him say as He spoke directly to my spirit (not an audible voice): *"The angel is assigned to you personally and is with you all the time.* ***You saw Me as I was when a man (the Son of Man), but you will see me as I am"*** (emphasis added). I will never forget that time in my life as it changed my relationship to God to one that was deeply personal. I have on other occasions seen angels and sensed angelic and spiritual activity around me. I know and often sense the angel assigned to me. From that time forward I had other visions, but not all of them were open and of such magnitude as that one. I continued to grow spiritually and recognized even more the prophetic gift in my life.

Some years later in 1996, I was ministering in Ashkelon, Israel. There were three of us on that trip, and the Lord had us walking and interceding in that city on a daily basis for three months. About two weeks before we were to head back to the States, I was finishing my daily prayer walk and stepped up into the park where I would write notes and ponder what the Lord had shown and spoken to me. That day as I stepped up into the park, I walked into an open vision. Suddenly, I found myself standing in a wheat field so real that I felt as though I could reach out and touch the wheat. The field was not yet ripe for harvest but was very close. As I continued to observe the vision, I saw the Lord Jesus standing at the end of the field with His arms outstretched toward the wheat as if looking for the time of the harvest. Then, as suddenly as I stepped into the vision, I found myself seated on a park bench inquiring of the Lord as to the purpose of the vision. He told me three things which had significance over the following years.

- Pray for the raising up of prophetic, evangelistic teams in that city and all of Israel.
- Pray for intercessors to intercede for those teams as they are sent forth into that city and other parts of Israel.

Chapter 9 - Experiencing the Prophetic Realm

- Pray for the raising up of home church leaders (shepherds, pastors) in the city of Ashkelon as that was where He would meet with His people.

As I pondered these words, I realized that I had no idea what a prophetic, evangelistic team was. I also researched the promises for Ashkelon in the Scriptures and found only one significant word for what the Lord had shown and spoken that day. I found the following in Zephaniah 2:6-7:

The seacoast shall be pastures, with shelters for shepherds and folds for flocks. The coast shall be for the remnant of the house of Judah; they shall feed their flocks there; in the houses of Ashkelon, they shall lie down at evening. For the Lord their God will intervene (visit them), and return their captives (emphasis mine).

About a month later, we returned to our home base at a ministry in Charlotte, North Carolina. It was a Friday night, and we went to their School of the Spirit meeting where Bob Weiner was speaking to the students of the ministry school. He stated something like the following: "You students have one of the greatest tools for evangelism and that is the prophetic gift, as God knows the hearts of all people. This gift will be a mighty tool for evangelistic outreach. Next, you will need to have intercessory teams to pray for you as you go out to the streets. Finally, your home groups will be a place to disciple and pastor these new believers." After that meeting, I showed Bob my notes from the above vision a month earlier in Ashkelon. We were both amazed that God was setting a new course for His Church in evangelism. Since that time, many churches have adopted similar kinds of outreach teams to the lost and dying.

Another way God began to speak to me is somewhat controversial but we will test and confirm it with Scripture. This part of the seer gift in which the prophetic person sees the countenance of a known person on the one receiving the prophecy. This seeing will be either a glimpse in the spirit (like a mind picture) or an open vision as described above. Below are two examples:

I was in a meeting with a group of men and the leader of the meeting asked us to seek the Lord for a word for a person in the meeting. I focused on a young man seated directly across from me. I asked the Lord what He desired to speak to this young man. Immediately, I saw the likeness of a mentor of mine projected onto this man's face. It was the face and countenance of my teaching mentor **James Edward** Fredrick (not his real last name). Then I saw in the Spirit this young man sitting at a desk in deep study and behind him was a library of many reference books. This all being a new thing for me, I pondered for a moment and said, "You remind me of my teaching mentor named James and I believe the Lord is showing me that you have a call to teach on your life and that you have a deep passionate desire to begin teaching God's Word. I see that you have a library of reference books at home, and you appear to be a man of diligent study of the Bible." Wow, I had just stepped out in greater faith than before and gave the word from a new perspective. The young man replied with tears in his eyes saying, "You don't realize what you have said. My name is **James**, but my friends call me **Ed** (**Edward** the middle name of my mentor). He continued by saying, "I have such a deep desire to teach God's Word to his people and the opportunity has not yet arrived for me to do that. And yes, I have a vast library of study Bibles and reference books at my home. This word confirms the things I believe God has called me to do."

Another time, I was at a retreat/conference of the ministry that ordained me. Again, we were asked by the leader to seek God for a word for any attendee. As I looked about the room, the Holy Spirit prompted my attention to another man. Looking at him in the Spirit, I saw the likeness of the former San Francisco Forty Niner quarterback **Steve Young**. Asking the Lord for the interpretation, the following came to me: *His name is* **Steve**, *and I have called him to a ministry with the* **young** *people in My church.* (I did ask him for his

Chapter 9 - Experiencing the Prophetic Realm

name to assure myself that I had heard God.) *He is my quarterback, and I am sending him the plays to use in raising up the young people of this generation.* When he heard the word, it was again another confirmation of what God was doing in his life.

To assure us that there is a scriptural reference for seeing in the Spirit like this I remembered 2 Kings 2:9-15,

> *And so it was when they crossed over, that Elijah said to Elisha, "ask what may I do for you, before I am taken away from you?" Elisha said, "Please let **a double portion of your spirit be upon me**." So he said, "You have asked a hard thing. Nevertheless, if you see me when I am taken from you, it shall be so for you, but if not, it shall not be so." Then it happened, as they continued on and talked, that suddenly a chariot of fire appeared with horses of fire, and separated the two of them; and Elijah went up by a whirlwind into heaven. And **Elisha saw it**, and he cried out "My father, my father, the chariot of Israel and its horsemen!" So he saw him no more. And he took hold of his own clothes and tore them into two pieces. He also took up the mantle of Elijah that had fallen from him, and went back and stood by the bank of the Jordan. Then he took the mantle of Elijah that had fallen from him, and struck the water, and said, "Where is the Lord God of Elijah?" And when he had struck the water, it was divided this way and that; and Elisha crossed over. Now when **the sons of the prophets who were from Jericho saw him, they said, "The spirit of Elijah rests on Elisha."** And came to meet him and bowed to the ground before him.*

We see here that the sons of the prophets from Jericho **saw the spirit of Elijah upon Elisha.** God can do anything beyond our natural senses in the prophetic spiritual realm. It was not that the sons of the prophets saw him part the waters, but *it specifically says that they saw the spirit of Elijah rest upon Elisha.*

UFO's in Roswell, New Mexico

I want to share a vision that my late wife, Gail, had that set us on another journey that we did not understand at the time of the adventure. During the time of her vision, we were both in training to hear and know the Lord's voice and this experience seemed odd to us as you will see. We had a time of prayer every Saturday morning, and during this period she saw in the Spirit the following: We were driving down a road from a mountainous area, and she saw large, high, rolling hills as we headed toward a city yet unknown. She saw a large warehouse building on the right and entering the city she saw a southwest style apartment house with turned wood bars on the windows. She saw Jesus standing in the window with a small group of people who seemed to be praying with Him. As we entered the city, she saw spaceships and then in high black letters she saw the words Roswell, New Mexico.

A short time later we were invited to minister at a friend's church in Denver, Colorado. We were short on money, but after a substantial offering from that meeting, we decided to drive south and east to Roswell to see if God had something for us to do in that city. As we approached Roswell, we were driving down from the mountains as in her vision and saw some rolling hills, which were similar to what she saw. So, we began to look for the red warehouse building as we drew closer to Roswell. We saw some similar looking buildings, but they were not the one she saw in the vision. We began to wonder if we had missed it and were on a wild goose chase.

Next, we decided to seek after the southwest style apartment with the turned wood posts on the windows. We went to the local Chamber of Commerce to ask for specific apartments of that style. Our journey lasted several hours, and none of those we saw were like the apartment in Gail's vision. Finally, we headed toward the abandoned Air Force base where they had built some apartments. On our way, there we passed the UFO Museum reminding us that she had seen flying saucers in her vision experience. Was this another clue that we were hearing God? Entering the Air Base, we realized the apartments were not even close to what she had seen in the vision.

Discouraged, we drove through the base and came to a stop sign. Gail was disappointed and her head was nearly in her lap. Surprised, I told her to look at the street sign, and she hesitated, wondering why that was important. The street sign read "Gail Harris Street." Seeing this sign was the first encouragement that helped her know that she had heard from God. But what did it mean? We turned left on that street only to find an abandoned church with the windows boarded up. This building was another sign because we felt part of our call was to restore God's church back to its original intent. Driving on, we saw a car parked in a driveway that was exactly like the car Gail had before we were married. In dreams, cars can represent ministries. Seeing all these things was encouraging, but why were we in that city? It took several months for us to realize that this was the beginning of learning to follow God. Finally, we realized that it would take great trust to follow Him in the new and various ways He was speaking to us.

As a closing point to this vision, the building that we currently meet in is a warehouse on the right side of the highway as you approach the foothills just West of our location in Colorado. It was several years before we found this place, and finally, we realized this was another part of her vision.

Trance

Trance is another type of vision we can experience. Trances are mentioned at least five times in the Scriptures. I would place a trance in the category of a visionary experience because one is seeing in the Spirit. Numbers 24:16 gives us a Hebrew perspective of a trance, and it is translated as *"the utterance of him who hears the words of God, and has knowledge of the Most High,* **who sees the vision of the Almighty, who falls down, with eyes wide open."**

A Paradigm Shift of Prophetic Revelation

In the New Covenant writings, we see the word "trance" given the following definition: The Greek word ***ekstasis*** is translated as amazement, astonishment, and trance also means ***a displacement of the mind.*** The use of the word *ekstasis* as *trance* is used three times in the New Covenant in Acts 10:10; 11:5; 22:17. In Acts 10:10 Peter fell into a trance *"Then he became very hungry and wanted to eat; and while they made ready,* ***he fell into a trance."***

It strikes me that the first time I experienced a trance I ***fell face down on the floor into an ecstatic state of vision.*** Or we might say as "one caught up in the Spirit." During a time of fasting and praying for a direction, I walked into the living room where my wife was praying, and I immediately felt a heaviness of the Lord's presence. I stopped and suddenly fell onto the floor face down, and the Spirit took me to the foot of the Cross. I was aware for a moment that my body was on the floor, but my spirit and mind were in a different place. I could see Jesus on the Cross and heard men cursing Him. I was without a doubt in that place in the Spirit. I saw clearly the crown of thorns on His head and unlike an artist's rendering, His head was bleeding profusely. I saw the pain and agony on His face and the pressure of the weight of His body pulling on the spikes in His wrist and feet. When I heard the men cursing and mocking Him, I cried out in the Spirit with a loud anguished, "No!" Then the blood from His wounds fell upon my hands. I felt the pain and knew at that moment two things: my sin was responsible for His death because His blood was on my hands. Then, at nearly the same time, I knew His blood cleansed me from all sin. Suddenly, just like a zoom lens on a camera, I found myself looking at the Cross from a greater distance. As I gazed upon the new scene in the vision, I saw an empty Cross. To the left of the Cross and slightly taller/larger than the Cross I saw the appearance of an enormous golden eagle. Again, like a camera lens, I zoomed away and suddenly I was drawn closer to see the eye of the eagle. The eagle's eye began to turn and rotate and in the pupil I saw the image of the glorified Christ as a bright and shining star. This experience led us to the ministry where we were

Chapter 9 - Experiencing the Prophetic Realm

to receive further training to send us out to Israel and Europe. The Cross and the eagle were similar to the logo of that ministry.

At another time in my life, I experienced something very similar, and I believe it also was a trance. I had been invited to speak at a friend's church and a Full Gospel Business Men's meeting in Denver, Colorado. I arrived at my friend's home late on a Friday evening and not yet prepared to speak at the Full Gospel meeting that next morning. I was up late that night and had nothing from the Lord to share except my testimony the following morning.

I awoke Saturday concerned that I had nothing to share, so I immediately dropped to my knees at the bedside and began to pray. Another "suddenly" and I was in the Spirit and in the meeting that would take place several hours later. I saw several things that were to happen (actually were happening in the ecstatic state of vision I was in at the moment). I saw a woman standing behind a long table with a small amount of food. She had a look on her face as if wondering why there was not more food on the table. In another moment, I saw two older men that looked exactly alike and they were talking to a younger man who was standing by a customized mini pickup truck. Then, I was taken into the office of what appeared to be a businessman who was an official in the Full Gospel Business Men's Association. I could see his face and that he was working on something for that association that had to do with the finances of that group. The next thing I knew, I got up to prepare for the breakfast meeting. Between the time I arrived at the meeting and my getting up from the bedside, I remembered nothing from the trance.

I arrived at the meeting about 15 minutes early and met the leaders and some of the folks there. We had breakfast, and I got up to speak still not sure exactly what I was going to say. After mumbling about my testimony, I suddenly saw the woman who was at the table in the trance. I told her that I had seen her in a vision that morning, and she was standing in front of a table that was lacking food. I asked her if that was a problem she was aware of and she said she was in charge of Operation Blessing in the Denver area, and they were short on their food stock for that month. We immediately prayed into that problem asking and believing God for a greater supply of food. As we continued to pray and minister, I saw one of the two men who were with the younger man and the pickup truck. He introduced his twin brother and the one who looked like him. I told them about the encounter I had seen with the younger man—only knowing that later that was to happen, and they would minister to this man. Wrapping up my time, I had several words of knowledge and some healing took place as we prayed for some of the folks.

After the meeting, I mentioned to my friend about the man in the office. I described him to a tee, and my friend responded knowing that this man was involved with the Full Gospel Business Men's Fellowship International finances for the area. I let him deal with that situation as I had no other information than what God had shown me in the trance.

Simple Words

The prophetic gift is used any time God gives you the opportunity. I will share a few meaningful words I had for folks that I was able to follow up on.

We had some friends over for dinner one evening, and they asked if they could bring a new couple for us to meet. Our response was "sure, bring them along."

After dinner that night, we gathered in the living area and began to talk and pray together. Our guest asked if we could pray for the folks they brought with them. I assured them that yes, we could and as we prayed I heard the word of the Lord for them to "follow the yellow brick road." There were other words given them that evening of which I know longer remember. Their circumstances were that they were moving geographically to a new state and had no idea where they would be living. When they got there, they lived in an apartment for a short time and then decided to build a home on some acreage near the city where they had moved. As they searched

Chapter 9 - Experiencing the Prophetic Realm

in nearby areas, they were led to a zone where land lots were available. Their quest seemed hopeless until they saw a street sign saying, "Yellow Brick Road." Suddenly they remembered the evening they received the word saying, "follow the yellow brick road." In the early evening as they proceeded up the yellow brick road, they saw what appeared to be a city of lights, like The Land of Oz in the movie *The Wizard of Oz*. It was, in fact, an oil refinery plant. Being on the yellow brick road and seeing the lights of the refinery were confirmation they were being led by the Holy Spirit to continue on that path. A short time later and some miles further they found the exact acreage they wanted. They bought it and later built their home there. They shared the story with their friends who later related it to me.

Another significant word happened in Charlotte, North Carolina. After church one Sunday afternoon, we invited our friend, Sue, to lunch. When we arrived at the restaurant, parked the car and started inside, I said to my wife and Sue, "Let's ask God for a word for our waitress." We all agreed, were seated, and began to pray with eyes wide open for a word for our waitress. Immediately, in the Spirit I saw her on a camping trip with several lady friends. I heard the Lord speak clearly in my spirit, "she has been running from Me because I am pursuing her." Clearly, I saw her and some friends setting up a tent at a camping site. He also showed me that she had been on a camping trip earlier that had been out of His will. When we all had a word from the Lord she approached the table to take our order, and I asked her, "So when are you going camping?" She immediately responded with, "We just got our days off for that trip this week. How did you know I was going camping?" Our friend Sue said to her, "The Lord told him!" The waitress began to tear up as I expounded that she had been running from God and that He loved her and said, "I am pursuing her because I love her, and I have called her to My purposes." Sue and my wife, Gail, also gave her some encouraging words. As we left the restaurant, the young woman came to us and said, "The next time you are in the restaurant, be sure to ask for my station."

A Paradigm Shift of Prophetic Revelation

God is not limited to the ways He speaks to his people. The greatest ways He speaks to us is through the Scriptures. I always remind prophetic people and students to consume the Word; meditate on it day and night. Knowing and studying the Word is vital for us because there He reveals His character, love, and nature to us. Every prophetic person should remember His promise to us: *"If you abide in Me, and My words abide in you, you will ask what you desire, and it shall be done for you. By this is My Father glorified, that you bear much fruit; so you will be My disciples"* (John 15:7-8).

The essence of experiencing and releasing God's intent in the prophetic realm is to bear much fruit of His Spirit. By that is our Father glorified, and by that are many in and out of the Kingdom of God blessed with His love, power, and intent for their lives. He lives to bring life to the dead!

Prayer

Father, I pray for all who read this book that they identify with the prophetic realm of the Spirit and seek to enter. May they be led by Your Spirit as You have led me all these years. I pray that You would grant them the desires of their hearts, knowing that You give us such desires as we diligently seek You and the deeper things of the prophetic realm. Help us be assured of Your timing and purpose as we move into the deep calling unto the deep.

Amen

Chapter 10

Practicing Prophecy in the Church

How is it then, brethren? Whenever you come together, each of you has a psalm, has a teaching, has a tongue, has a revelation, has an interpretation. Let all things be done for edification (1 Corinthians 14:26).

From the beginning of this book, we have examined the various ways in which we, as the Body of Christ, should prepare ourselves in the process of bringing prophecy to a greater maturity. Progressing to this standard should be the ultimate goal of every prophetic person. The goal should be to express ourselves prophetically in the love, nature, and character of the Godhead fully. Colossians 2:9-10 reminds me of His intent for all who believe: *"For in Him dwells all the fullness of the Godhead bodily; and you are complete in Him, who is the head of all principality and power."* Love, humility, and the integrity and character of God are the first and most important issues in the process of our prophetic development. To see a change in the world, change must first take place in the church. The prophetic ministry, being a voice of the heart and mind of God, must, in fact, have His life living fully and relationally in us.

When I was first involved in prophetic ministry, there were two camps of thought. One camp leaned more toward the seer aspect of prophecy, while the other was geared more toward what I call the *Nabi* (Hebrew for prophet) style where the Lord would prompt a word in their spirit and the speaker would follow the flow of the Holy Spirit with the remainder of the word. Much of this was by inspiration and impression.

On arriving in Colorado in 1998, we were asked by some friends to do a prophetic seminar on how to hear the voice of God. We agreed to do four weeks once a week. Nearly 40 people showed up who had no training in prophecy, prophetic ministry, or the various ways in which God speaks to His people. That was a first of many classes we did on prophecy and hearing God's voice. That first class lasted eight weeks because the students wanted more. Also, that was the beginning of our work and the planting of a church in the Denver Metro area.

Later that same year, I was introduced to a woman who came from the *Nabi* camp. I didn't know much about that style but felt we were to get together and share thoughts and experiences in prophetic ministry and how it functioned in our churches. A few months later, we were invited to a monthly meeting in Colorado Springs, just one hour south of Denver. The meeting was beneficial for both of us and we started doing meetings and events together and exchanged pulpits from time to time. What the fruit of those meetings bore was a trust that we were all a part of the Body of Christ and a long-lasting relationship exists with this prophetic friend to this day.

Building Teams

As we planted our first church in Golden, Colorado, we believed the Lord wanted us to have a prophetic emphasis as a church which included our worship. After prayer and much planning, we began to determine a protocol for the prophetic teams. The prerequisite for participating on prophetic teams was that the potential team members were required to go through our eight-week training course. The course is set up first to build Christ-like character in the student so that their identity is not about being a prophetic person but focuses primarily on their oneness in Christ. This is in conjunction with the

Chapter 10 - Practicing Prophecy in the Church

entire 70-page syllabus of instruction, application, and workshops. As we progressed toward building prophetic teams for our church, we discovered that folks from other churches were interested in our classes. Since that time of equipping prophetic people, our teams often consist of people from other churches who join us when we do special conferences and events. One conference we held included people from other churches in the area trained in our school—900 people attended. We had trained enough people, including our members, to have 15 teams cover the two-day event. We were pioneering something new in our city and region; something that all other like-minded churches were able to participate in to help bring change from the heart of God speaking in our area.

Our prophetic teams consist of three people who have successfully finished the eight-week prophetic training classes. We have one team leader and two trained people on a team. The team leader must be mature in the Lord, have a sound understanding of Scripture, and be able to work with people, keeping the team and the recipient on track. By that, I mean keeping the focus on prophecy, not teaching, healing, counseling, or deliverance. The team leader is responsible for the time limit in a conference setting and the time set for teams during a special event or normal after-service ministry time. The time limit can depend on the amount of people per the number of prophetic teams available.

Through years of practice and consistent prayer, we resolved to prophesy only for edification, exhortation, and comfort—no prophesying on relationships, marriages, divorce, or babies. The reason for this is that some prophecies are seen or heard in a symbolic sense—such as pregnancy, seeing two people come together in relationship, or hearing or seeing a marriage in the Spirit. Without proper training and protocol, those issues seen or heard symbolically could easily be misinterpreted as real situations where people could be misled into dangerous situations. Our purpose is to connect people with God through confirming words that carry the theme of edification, exhortation, and comfort (see 1 Corinthians 14:3).

A Paradigm Shift of Prophetic Revelation

In the characteristics of prophetic ministry speaking words of edification, exhortation, and comfort, we must have a clearer view not only of their meanings but their effect. The intent of edification is the love of God for His people. Edification in Greek is *oikodome*, which comes from *oikos,* meaning a home and *dome* or to build. God desires to build a home for Himself in the life of the believer through prophetic words. *Oikodome* means the act of building figuratively and spiritually with the structure of God's intent, which is the promotion of spiritual growth. Edification, then, is spoken in prophecy to build up a person, local body, or an area of Christian life and ministry. God's desire is to build in us the strength and life of His Son through prophetic speaking. Edification is part of God's love to build up strong believers unto the measure of the stature of the fullness of Christ. Exhortation also has its roots in the love, nature, and character of God. In Greek, the word *parakaleo* was used primarily to call to a person, to admonish, exhort, to urge one to pursue some course of conduct (always prospective, looking to the future). Many in the Body of Christ need to hear God admonishing, encouraging, and exhorting them to Kingdom conduct and action. To exhort is to bring the highest possible encouragement into the life of the recipient of the prophetic word.

We often think of comfort as consoling someone. However, from the Greek word *paramuthia,* comfort can be any address made for the purpose of persuading, arousing, stimulating, or calming someone through prophetic ministry. By definition and use, prophetic comfort has its roots in the very heart of God's love and care for His people.

Because we are discussing the act of speaking prophetically, we must pursue a deeper understanding of the prophetic purpose, perspective, disciplines, virtues, and characteristics of prophetic speaking not just in words, but through the character and nature of the person speaking as well as those receiving.

Chapter 10 - Practicing Prophecy in the Church

Developing Prophetic Protocol

In the 50+ years that I have been a believer I have watched the church move into one transition after another. We must realize that today's church is in another significant change. Recognizing change should stir us to look for various possible protocols needed for our time. Protocol is defined as correct diplomatic behavior. This discipline needs to be set up in the different ways, places, and times where prophecy is given. We should look at it from personal, local, regional, and national levels. The regional and national levels can best be served and directed by apostolic and prophetic leaders using internet social media and emails specifically aimed at communicating God's purposes for that region. Local area protocols will necessarily bring local church leaders together who engage in prophecy. They would operate in a similar manner as the council at Jerusalem written in Acts Chapter 15. Once this council determines what should be shared about the prophecy concerned, then local prophetic ministers or elders could deliver the word to the local body in their particular area of the city or region. The development of such councils remains as a pioneering effort and desperately needed for the Church at large.

In the local church, we should have a protocol for prophecy that takes place during our meetings and at a designated time for sharing revelations and prophecies. Other designated times would be events or time frames for prophetic team ministry. Setting protocols in place will not work without prior training in prophetic speaking and ministry, which should include sessions on protocol.

In Scripture, Paul gives us a glance at protocol in the early church:

> *But if all prophesy and an unbeliever or an uninformed person comes in, he is convinced by all, he is convicted by all. And thus the secrets of his heart are revealed; so falling down on his face he will worship God and report that God is truly among you" (1 Corinthians 14:24-25).*

A Paradigm Shift of Prophetic Revelation

What can we glean from this Scripture? Prophecy in our meetings has the unction to change the hearts of the hearers toward the love and power of God. The word of prophecy reports that God is in your midst, and that sets an evangelistic tone in your local church meeting.

For the sake of the question in our meetings of when is it appropriate to allow prophecy, we can look at another statement by the apostle Paul. *"How is it then, brethren?* **Whenever you come together***, each of you has a psalm, has a teaching, has a tongue, has a revelation, has an interpretation. Let all things be done for edification"* (1 Corinthians 14:26, emphasis added). My point is: What is the appropriate time for prophecy? Most churches, including my own, have selected to do this during our worship. But is this the best time for prophecy? Paul says, "whenever you come together." After years of seeing prophecy activated during worship in many churches, I have to ask the question, Is this the best time for us to prophesy? Does it interrupt our time of real worship to God? Or is prophecy a naturally supernatural spiritual flow in worship? From personal experience and talking with a handful of other leaders, prophecy seems to flow with the theme of the meeting from preparatory intercession into worship and often into the message of the meeting.

Before my pastoring days, I was involved in pre-meeting intercession and the Holy Spirit would often reveal to the intercessors what God would be doing in the meetings. I have seen it happen numerous times. Often those involved with intercession or personal time with the Lord would experience a common theme across the nation and sometimes the world. Prophecy then can occur "whenever you come together." It is a part of the flow of God's Spirit revealing His heart for a time, season, or coming event.

The apostle Paul addressed another issue of protocol in his letter to the Corinthian church. This issue has to do with the order of prophetic speaking in a local or even a regional meeting or conference where allowed. Again, this is the theme of "whenever you come together."

Chapter 10 - Practicing Prophecy in the Church

*Let two or three prophets speak, and let the others judge. But if anything is revealed to another who sits by, let the first keep silent. For you can all prophesy one by one, that **all may learn** and **all may be encouraged**. And the spirits of the prophets are subject to the prophets (1 Corinthians 14:29-32, emphasis added).*

In our church, we approach prophetic speaking in our meetings as such: During our worship time, we have an open microphone for prophecy, songs, hymns, and spiritual songs. Our people know that we prophesy only for edification, exhortation, and comfort during that time. We announce to any visitors that this is the purpose of prophecy in our meetings. If visitors, including affiliate prophetic ministers, have a prophetic word, they must first speak it to the designated leadership to judge. They may be allowed to give it, our leader may give it, or we may hold it for further judging and weighing. We let them know that in doing this they have obeyed and delivered what they believed God has given them, and the responsibility for judging now lies with the local leaders. This action agrees with the Scripture above, *"let two or three prophets speak and let the others judge."*

Along with the Scripture above is the matter that the responsibility for prophecy and judging is subject to the spirits of the prophetic people speaking (see 1 Corinthians 14:29-32). The words "subject to" mean *under the authority or control of, or owing allegiance to another*. Prophetic speakers should honor others, not interrupt another, and take responsibility for what they speak in the meeting. The gift of prophecy requires control and accountability on the part of the prophetic speaker to avoid confusion in the meeting. Speaking prophetically in this way is a vital part of establishing a biblically-based protocol that can be practiced in our meetings today.

Note that this protocol is addressed to those who prophesy—meaning those gifted in simple prophecy, prophetic ministry, or those in the office of a prophet. The order is given that they speak one by one honoring and respecting the other prophetic people in the meeting. It is implied that those who are gifted, instructed and engaged in prophecy do the judging. Judging would include the elders and local leaders involved in a meeting where prophecy is released. Paul's letter is addressed to the church at Corinth and included in Scripture for our instruction, doctrine, correction, or reproof (see 2 Timothy 3:16). Therefore, we can determine that it is an applicable principle for today's Church and Kingdom.

If the word is for the corporate Body, the region, the nation, or world, we encourage our people to submit it to the leadership for judging before releasing it to that group. Most individuals who have been through prophetic training are comfortable with that process and know its biblical foundation.

The above principles are not to be considered a letter of the law but a standard of protocol for an order of peace and avoidance of confusion in any meeting (see 1 Corinthians 14:29-33).

Concerning Prophetic Teams

We have prophetic teams consisting of students who have completed our prophetic school who prophesy over local and regional people who come to our Jeremiah 33:3 meetings once a month. Jeremiah 33:3 night is a monthly meeting that is open to all local churches in the area to come and receive a personal prophetic word from our teams. The team members may be from our fellowship or other churches in the area, but one requirement is that they have permission from their local leadership to participate with us in prophetic team ministry. Our teams are set up to prophesy personally over individuals, families, or leaders who attend those meetings. Primarily, our standards are for edification, exhortation, and comfort. Again, we do not give any corrective words or prophecies concerning marriage, relationships, divorces, or babies. These standards come from prayer and Scripture concerning these

Chapter 10 - Practicing Prophecy in the Church

types of meetings. Our desire is to connect people with God to encourage, confirm, and release spiritual freedom and growth.

Protocol for Visiting Prophetic Ministers

Protocol for visiting prophetic ministers would agree with the standards of protocol addressed above. Additionally, this must be established through a relationship between the leaders and visiting prophet or prophetic minister. It should always stay within the scriptural boundaries agreed upon between the hosting ministry and the visiting speakers. For purposes of clarity, Kingdom doctrine, and the realm of the supernatural, biblical standards should be in place as to allow the Holy Spirit to lead in only those things that glorify Jesus and the Father. These standards are critical for the times in which we live as Jesus states: *"For false christs, and false prophets will rise and show great signs and wonders to deceive, if possible, even the elect"* (Matthew 24:24). Much of the church today is looking for great signs and wonders and often searching for a prophetic minister for those things to occur. For this reason, it is vital for those in a position of leadership to know those who labor among them, ensuring that the Kingdom is advanced and the one true King Jesus is glorified. (For more on this subject, see my book: *The Face of Prophecy: Determining the Truth*, published in 2011.)

Practicing Prophecy

I have attended several Charismatic and Evangelical services over the years and found perhaps a handful of people who had the freedom to prophesy during a meeting time. Often and for some unknown reason, prophecy is allowed only during the worship time of the meeting. Then our religious tradition takes over, and we shut it down and proceed with offerings, announcements, and the primary speaker of the day.

A Paradigm Shift of Prophetic Revelation

Is this biblical? Did the Corinthian church need correction regarding this according to the apostle Paul's writings? Are scriptural writings often avoided in regard to this? My intent here is not to be controversial, but I hear so much about how we must follow biblical protocol in our meetings. Let's take for example some things recorded about the meetings at Corinth.

> *Therefore tongues are for a sign, not to those who believe but for unbelievers; but prophesying is not for unbelievers but for those who believe. Therefore if the whole church comes together in one place, and all speak with tongues, and there come in those who are uninformed or unbelievers, will they not say that you are out of your mind? But if all prophesy, and an unbeliever or an uninformed person comes in, he is convinced by all, he is convicted by all. And thus the secrets of his heart are revealed; and so, falling down on his face, he will worship God and report that God is truly among you (1 Corinthians 14:22-25).*

As a local church here in Colorado, we have been practicing prophecy for over 16 years. In that time, we have found the need for structured freedom in our meetings. In the above example, I ask the question concerning prophecy being done only in the time of worship—is this biblical or man-made protocol? Having been in other churches where prophecy is done only during worship, it seems to be good and in order. However, in the above Scriptures, Paul appears to be indicating there is great freedom within structure and authority.

I want to suggest here that the leadership of the early church was in transition, learning how to oversee meetings where the things (*gifts*) of the Spirit were moving in their midst. Somehow in the excitement of the *gifts* being in place, matters got out of control and produced confusion. I see much of the same thing happening in some churches today where the *gifts* are allowed to operate without training and protocol. Training and protocol are not a major part

Chapter 10 - Practicing Prophecy in the Church

of discipling new believers as that deals more with the principle doctrines of Christ. After establishing gifts and callings in the discipling process, then it is time to "equip the saints for service" (see Ephesians 4:12). At that time, apostles, prophets, evangelists, pastors, and teachers take the discipled "saints" and equip them for service in their particular gifts and callings. This process takes place so that the Body is not easily swayed and *"carried about with every wind of doctrine, by the trickery of men, in the cunning craftiness of deceitful plotting"* (Ephesians 4:14).

Paul made it clear in these scenarios that all believers with various *gifts* are encouraged to participate. But without established discipleship and equipping we are left with the ideas of men often in the tradition of their pet doctrines of safety and control. However, when we read and study his intent for such services in 1 Corinthians 14:26, we find that multiple prophetic gifts were present, and everyone was participating toward the sole purpose of bringing edification to the church. I have yet to see this done during a time of worship.

But where in Scripture does it give us instruction to prophesy during worship? Order overrides confusion when the following things occur:

> *If anyone speaks in a tongue, let there be two or at the most three, each in turn, and let one interpret. But if there is no interpreter, let him keep silent in the church, and let him speak to himself and to God" (1 Corinthians 14:27-28).*

Tongues without interpretation have no value to the church meeting. Speaking in tongues with no interpretation should be done quietly, not bringing attention to oneself, but talking to himself and to God. Tongues also edify the speaker in this case. We encourage speaking in tongues in our meetings, knowing our people and knowing their gifts. Often, certain individuals will have an interpretation. (There is a particular *gift* of the Spirit called the interpretation of tongues, see 1 Corinthians 12:10).

A Paradigm Shift of Prophetic Revelation

In like manner, there is a protocol in place when prophesying in our meetings. Paul also makes this clear with the purpose of *"Let all things be done decently and in order"* (1 Corinthians 14:40). The order of prophecy is described here as,

> Let two or three prophets speak, and let the others judge. But if anything is revealed to another who sits by, let the first keep silent. For you may all prophesy one by one, that all may learn and all may be encouraged. And the spirits of the prophets are subject to the prophets. **For God is not the author of confusion but of peace, as in all the churches of the saints** (1 Corinthians14:29-33, emphasis added).

Prophecy, like all other *gifts* of the Spirit, has an order and purpose that carries the intent of God in our meetings. The order is that two or three prophets speak. I want to note here that I believe that the prophetic speaking of two or more will be on the same theme of God's heart for that particular meeting. Secondly, if necessary at the time, *"let the others judge,"* meaning that they are to examine, investigate, search the heart, and determine the truth and intent of the prophetic words spoken. The Greek word translated *judge* here is *anakrino* indicating examination. By "others" I believe this refers to other prophets, prophetic people in the meeting or those designated by the leadership to judge the words at that time. This judging is necessary to fully understand the intent and purpose of the prophecy when two or three prophets speak a similar theme. It may also refer to 1 Corinthians 14:30: *"But if anything is revealed to another who sits by,* (implying one who has a revelation/interpretation of what the word means), *let the first keep silent."* Paul further notes that the speaking of prophecy be *one by one that all in the meeting may learn and be encouraged.* We are not talking about a doctrinal teaching to be taught—rather the theme of God's heart for all hearing the prophecy.

Chapter 10 - Practicing Prophecy in the Church

Additionally, and definitely as important is the *"the spirits of the prophets are subject to the prophets"* (1 Corinthians 14:32). Prophets being subject to their spirit has much more meaning than most of the church understands. We know from previous chapters that God is Spirit and that He speaks to our spirit (see Nehemiah 9:30). Therefore, prophecy is something of the substance of the Spirit of God given to those God calls and equips specifically for the work of that ministry in the Kingdom. God speaks to His prophets by His Spirit in them. In this covenant, the Spirit of God dwells in us, and we become one with Him just as He and Jesus are One so are we one with them (see John 17:20-26.) Thus, when we speak a prophetic word, our spirit is subject to the oneness of God's Holy Spirit within us. Prophecy then is subject to the control and responsibility of the possessor.

Finally, with a protocol of biblical knowledge and purpose, peace takes place over confusion when God is the author of all things done in our meetings for edification. Paul makes his point clear that this is not his idea:

> *If anyone thinks himself to be a prophet or spiritual, let him acknowledge that the things I write to you are the commandments of the Lord. But if anyone is ignorant, let him be ignorant. Therefore, brethren, desire earnestly to prophesy, and do not forbid to speak with tongues. Let all things be done decently and in order (1 Corinthians 14:37-40).*

There is a great responsibility for the prophetic person and his/her spirit to be subject to what Paul writes as the commandments of the Lord. Prophetic people should never take this portion of Scripture lightly as a spokesperson of God's heart.

What is written here for us is specific apostolic nature and function. The apostolic role of Paul over the Corinthian church was such that he saw the need for order and protocol during the service to the Lord. God gave the *gifts*, but men had little or no instruction as to their use, and thus confusion and chaos occurred where decency and order were the heart of God.

It's hard to call oneself a church and practice prophecy and other spiritual gifts in a setting of worship or any time designated in a service to the Lord. When new folks come as visitors, they either love the freedom or fear it, thinking it is not proper to do such things in a worship setting. I am reminded and often share the Scripture where Paul says, *"Pursue love, and desire spiritual gifts, but especially that you may prophesy"* (1 Corinthians 14:1).

Some visitors are alarmed by dancing, flagging, and lifting up holy hands. How do we develop a protocol with freedom and structure around these kinds of actions in our worship? The apostle seems to believe there is a freedom with structure in our coming together. He suggests the following (I think it is justified to say it here again as a challenge about our worship to God in our meetings): *"How is it then brethren?* **Whenever you come together,** *each of you has a psalm, has a teaching, has a tongue, has a revelation, has an interpretation.* **Let all things be done for edification"** (1 Corinthians 14:26). Everything that takes place within a biblical context allows us that freedom in our service of worship. The structure comes in how we put things together for edification—that is to build up the worship to our God, who honored David in his dance because David's intent was to honor the joy and freedom he enjoyed in knowing His God (see 2 Samuel 6:14-16).

We develop a protocol for prophecy in a like manner. God does not require a religious rhetoric or set of traditional rules for worship to Him. We are to worship Him in Spirit and truth. Our worship, no matter what it entails, should always be vertically loving Him and bringing our heart to His heart relationally. We worship in Spirit and truth via the Holy Spirit who dwells in us, and the truth of Himself living in us. He loves us, and His heart is this: *"Now the Lord is the Spirit; and where the Spirit of the Lord is there is liberty"* (2 Corinthians 3:17).

Chapter 10 - Practicing Prophecy in the Church

Practicing Words of Warning

Often the Body of Christ and some individuals need to hear a word of warning from the Lord, which may at times include leaders in the local Body. A protocol for giving this type of prophecy must be developed in the love and intent of God to protect those receiving and delivering this kind of word. A word of warning is not meant to be a disciplinary word but a word of love and wisdom to keep us on track and in God's safety zone of freedom.

The Old Covenant prophets often gave words of warning to the kings of Israel concerning enemy attacks, incorrect Kingdom decisions or ruthless and fraudulent people who had crept into leadership. Some of the wiser kings of Israel would seek a prophet when they needed to hear from God concerning a Kingdom issue. Others in the Old Covenant received warning dreams which required prophetic interpretation. Men like the prophet Daniel and Joseph were called to help with dreams and interpretation.

In the New Covenant, the apostle Paul was warned by a prophetic group in Tyre to not go up to Jerusalem. As he continued his journey toward Caesarea, he stayed at the house of Phillip, who had four daughters who prophesied. A short time later, the prophet Agabus came from Jerusalem to Phillip's house and suddenly Paul was surrounded by prophetic people. In a prophetic act, Agabus picked up Paul's belt and prophesied that the Jews in Jerusalem would bind the owner of that belt. God in His sovereign grace had warned Paul of impending danger more than once.

The Lord is very aware of the times we need to be informed and, in His love and compassion for our welfare, often sends a prophetic minister to deliver that word. Several years ago, my late wife, Gail, and I were planning a trip to Israel. During that time, I received several dreams that warned of impending danger on this journey. At the same time, we were being encouraged to go by the leaders of the ministry of which we were a part. Feeling pushed by the strength of the vision and mission, we missed the intent of the warning dreams.

A Paradigm Shift of Prophetic Revelation

Also, due to overwhelming circumstances, we decided to go. Missing God's warning was a mistake on our part. While we were crossing the Atlantic on an airplane, a prophetic friend in Austria had a crucial warning dream concerning the same thing I had received about our trip to Israel. The moment our Austrian friends picked us up at the airport, they told us about the dream and gave us a word of warning that this was not the time for us to go. The warning of impending danger was considered, judged, and interpreted that we would meet with such opposition that our purpose for going would fail. We were called to minister prophetic training there, but the wrong people were in place for what we were called to do in Israel. It was a people and timing issue, and we would have missed it if the Lord had not graciously warned us not to go at that time.

The word of warning was correct and the timing to go was wrong. While in Austria, we canceled our trip and returned to America. After returning to the US, we discovered that the people in Israel were not open to prophetic training in the city of Ashkelon. There was much opposition, and the wrong team was in place for our mission. It took some time for us to adjust to our mistake. We learned to heed prophetic warnings, judge them, and move accordingly. Two years later, the Lord made the way to go very clear, and the right people were in place. The timing was right with everything in order, and we accomplished that which the Lord had called us to do in Israel.

Just as in correction and direction, words of warning are best given and received through the proper protocol of relationship between those giving and those receiving. These words always need to be judged and will often require us to adjust our plans or repent for not obeying or listening to that which God may have given us personally concerning that situation. Finally, we must remember that the Lord gives warnings to keep us safe, in His will, or on the right path to Kingdom works of righteousness.

Chapter 10 - Practicing Prophecy in the Church

Words Concerning Direction

When giving a directive prophecy, our responsibility must come from a time of pondering and giving deep thought to that word. The prophetic speaker should spend a considerable amount of time asking God specifics about timing and content before delivering a directive word. I do not recommend giving a word concerning a change of direction through a spontaneous prophecy. However, there may be times when that will be a general prophecy of confirming a direction for which an individual or a local body has been praying.

A directive word will bring a sense of newness and refreshing about God's goal for an individual or corporate body. To move or journey in a direction, one needs a map, weather report, and road or flying conditions, all from which we can pursue a plan of action. A directive prophecy should be delivered similarly to giving a road map to a person beginning a journey for which they have received only partial directions. This could apply to one who has gotten off God's course of direction for their lives or ministry. A prophetic word of guidance will have encouragement as well as particular interpretation and application for the new direction.

I believe that God wants directive prophecies to be given in the context of relationships both individually and corporately with those in the body receiving that word. By that I mean we must know those (relationally) who labor among us and esteem them very highly in love for their work's sake (see 1 Thessalonians 5:12-13). Corporate words should always have an order of protocol. That is why we see a principle set in Scripture where God speaks to the prophet, the prophet speaks to leaders, and finally the leaders judge the word and consider how it is conveyed to the body. A directive word to a corporate body will be given because of the relationship between the prophet and the leadership. By relationship, I mean a history of knowing and trusting those with whom you labor in Christ on a regular basis. The word of direction is given because of the relationship through prayer between the prophet and the leadership team. That word will either confirm direction prayed for, or be a change of current course in that body.

In judging a directive word, there will be evidence of the deep relationship of God with the prophet and the prophet with the leadership. That relationship will be built upon years of trust and work together in accountability to the Lord and to one another, living out of the commandment in 1 John 4:21, *"that he who loves God must love his brother also."*

We need some caution concerning personal directive words. First, in this current covenant we all have the indwelling Holy Spirit. Because of that, we can hear God personally as to His specific plans for our lives, which at times will include direction. But to hear Him, we must be willing to listen and be familiar with the various ways in which He speaks to us. Therefore, we should be cautious about giving direction, inquiring of the Lord for confirmation of a word that He may have already spoken to the person about a direction in their lives.

For example, I have at times seen in the Spirit someone called to a mission field in another nation. As I quietly listen to the Spirit, I ask the Lord how to present this word with the understanding that this is a call, not a commissioning to go now. So, I may say after inquiring of the Lord, "I believe the Lord is calling you to… and you are in a season of preparation. You will need to pray and draw close, asking Him for further instructions concerning the timing of that call." When I have done this in that matter, I have taken the prophetic responsibility only to confirm what God has already spoken to them. Another example might be seeing them called before they have heard from God. Both words require faith on the part of the prophetic speaker. When I see the call, the prophecy will be less directive and more persuasive and comforting such as, "I see that you have a powerful call on your life to those of your native culture. God is placing this call in your heart now, and I believe He will confirm it to you over time."

Chapter 10 - Practicing Prophecy in the Church

Again, our responsibility in giving such a word comes more quickly because of our time in preparation for prophetic ministry. Once delivered, the responsibility then becomes the recipients to judge and pray over that word until it is confirmed or comes to pass.

What About Corrective Words?

New Covenant prophetic ministry is sensitive, so we must be careful when giving a corrective prophecy. But there is a time, place, and often a need for it in today's church. Giving prophetic correction is only speaking God's intent to bring biblical and godly correction to a person, local body or Kingdom entity. A corrective prophetic word should not be given through conventional, inspirational prophecy; rather it requires time to pray over and meditate on the burden the Lord has revealed to the prophetic person. It should never be given publicly in a corporate meeting. It may even require rehearsal of the word before giving it. Most New Covenant prophets in Scripture frequently traveled, so they had time to meditate and consider the word before the delivery. The order of protocol was God to the prophet, the prophet to the leaders, and the leaders to the people. Within that time frame, the prophet should consider the content of the word, the heart of God, and the benefit to the Kingdom condition. That just means correction will also have the standards of New Covenant prophecy, edification, exhortation, and comfort. God's greatest desire is to build the Kingdom, but often things must be corrected before the Kingdom purpose can fulfill the Lord's intent of correction.

Understanding the time and place for corrective words is vital to a church or ministry. The prophetic minister's relationship with God is essential for the delivery and acceptance of corrective words. If the prophetic minister's life is not right with God's intent, they will tend to bring a part of their ideas or thoughts in the word. In bringing corrective prophecy, the minister's lifestyle must have a history of a high standard of godliness. We must examine the Scriptures where this type of ministry took place.

A Paradigm Shift of Prophetic Revelation

I am reminded again in 1 Thessalonians 5:12, Paul urges us to know those who labor among us. This statement is more than casually identifying a person; it has to do with building a working relationship with them so that we can recognize when we are in agreement with one another. Fellowship in the Body of Christ is more than having casual relationships. It involves transparency and joint participation in a community. *Koinonia* is the Greek word used in the New Covenant for this kind of openness, trust, and intimacy within the Christian community. The apostles urged us toward relationships built on loving one another and esteeming others more highly than ourselves.

The prophetic ministry plays a vital role in building relationships because it encourages, exhorts, and edifies the body. It is in the building of relationships in the body where *koinonia* becomes the hands and heart of leadership. Leaders in the church must develop trust, openness, and intimacy with one another that is a demonstration of a Christ-like community. Seasoned prophetic men and women are called to be a part of the Kingdom dynamics of spiritual growth that Paul describes in Ephesians 4. Trust built over time helps prophetic ministers to be accepted as part of the community. The church will begin to mature because another joint connects within God's Body. A joint makes an actual connection to other parts of the body.

When connecting relationships upon love and trust, the community of believers begins to mature. As we grow in maturity and confidence, we can more easily hear and judge corrective prophecy from the prophets with which we have a relationship. Where corrective prophecies are judged and accepted upon the building of mature relationships, then the needed corrections are quickly dealt with in the Kingdom community.

Corrective prophecy will never bring a new doctrine beyond that which is biblically established. It may, however, build on established doctrine to bring forth spiritual growth in the community and its leaders. A much-excused doctrine in the church today is the doctrine of offense that Jesus gave us in Matthew 18:15-20. We seldom experience the use of this teaching of Jesus because immature people see it as a confrontation. The idea of a battle is fear-based rather than love-based. I was recently involved in this kind of activity where people left a fellowship because of offense toward the leaders. Nothing was said to the leaders until much gossip and damaging hearsay was experienced. The leaders then sought prophetic counsel with those with whom they had a long-term relationship. After weeks of meetings and misunderstandings, a prophetic word was given by a prophetic minister that was present. The word was simply, "third party offense is gossip, and we must go back to the doctrine of offense in Matthew 18." This Scripture is a corrective prophecy concerning misuse of biblical doctrine. Once that took place among those with the offense, the community could then begin to move forward in love for one another. All misunderstanding was dealt with in love and concern for the whole community.

Corrective prophecy may also deal with issues of sin in the Body. It should never be spoken publicly but only within a council of responsible leaders who weigh and judge the word.

It could also bring correction for a needed change of activity for a local church or community. For example, it could change traditional business into a powerful dynamic move of the Holy Spirit to bring change to a community, region, or nation.

When a seasoned prophetic minister in a relationship with a community delivers a corrective prophecy, Jesus Christ is glorified, and the result of the word is life and peace.

Last Words

Prophecy in the local church today is ongoing, and I believe the Spirit of God continues to upgrade those called and commissioned to prophesy. God is building in us His love, nature, character, and integrity all for the purpose and intent of His heart for the church to release a pure and holy prophetic word for these last days, which we are rapidly entering.

A Paradigm Shift of Prophetic Revelation

Prayer

Father, we come before You as sons declaring Your Word, which states,

> And it shall come to pass in the last days, says God, That I will pour out My Spirit on all flesh; your sons and your daughters shall prophesy, your young men shall see visions, your old men will dream dreams, and on My menservants and on My maidservants I will pour My Spirit in those days; and they shall prophesy. I will show wonders in heaven above and signs in the earth beneath; blood and fire and vapor of smoke. The sun shall be turned into darkness, and the moon into blood, before the coming of the great and awesome day of the Lord, and it shall come to pass that whoever calls on the name of the Lord shall be saved (Acts 2:17-21; Joel 2:28-32).

CHAPTER 10 - PRACTICING PROPHECY IN THE CHURCH

BOOKS BY GOLDEN EAGLE MINISTRIES

In the Face of Prophecy
by Rich Harris
In the coming days, it will be essential that the body of Christ know and understand the dynamics of prophecy, prophets, and their purpose and function in the church and world today. As we draw closer to times of darkness and chaos in the world, there will arise many who claim to know God, predict the future, demonstrate great power, and give prophetic words that many long to hear. Some will be God's true prophetic voices, others will not. It is important that we be able to discern, understand, and deal with prophecy including those that are true, false, and those given by immature people. Rich carefully walks us throught he scriptural basis of prophecy, its nature and proper administration, and shows us how to determine the truth about prophecy.

ISBN 978-0-9785398-2-5 | $14.95

Visit www.LivingWordEvents.org
GoldenEaglePublishing/Books

Send checks to:
Golden Eagle Publishing
11413 W I-70 Frontage Road, North
Wheat Ridge, CO 80033
Call with a Credit Card: 303-989-2208

Prayer Psalms
Compiled by Ephraim & Rimona Frank

In the early 1970's, after being filled with the Holy Spirit, the Psalms became a wonderful source of inspiration, hope, encouragement, comfort, and exhortation for Ephraim in his newly found faith. He soon discovered that the words of the Psalms were revealing his heart-felt needs and at the same time made known an Almighty Creator and Father, whose very nature fulfilled every aspect of those needs. Consequently, Ephraim began to pray the Psalms in first person singular. In 1978 he moved to Israel and began learning the Hebrew language.

With the help of his native born Israeli wife, Rimona, he learned that his Heavenly Father had many names and that each of those names fit man's many complex needs. Ephraim incorporated those names as he was "praying the Psalms." These prayers are now available to inspire and encourage many.

Book comes with corresponding CD of the entire glossary with all the names of God spoken in Hebrew and English.
ISBN 0-9785398-1-8 $14.95 USD

Prophetic Evangelism
By Rich Harris

Prophetic evangelism is a worldwide coming move of God born from various prophetic and evangelisitc streams. Within these streams the Holy Spirit blows on His fiery forge tempering and hammering strategic tools of weaponry for the harvest of this age. This fully equipped army is illustrated through the words of Peter and the prophet Joel. Fulfillment of this prophecy began 2000 years ago when God's Spirit gave birth to the New Covenant church and continues *until the day of darkness* for "...many successive generations" (Joel 2:2 NKJV). As our generation hears God's voice, we must discard our own methods and programs and take up the spiritual weapons He is forming in the various streams of His eternal church.
$8.00 USD (currently out of print)

Gateway to Reconciliation
By Gail Harris
A true story of the love of God for His people, the Jews, as told to us by Pastor Helmuth and Uli Eiwen as they lived it.
$5.00 USD

Healing Earthbound Eagles
By Rodney Kingstone
In these days God is using the gift of prophecy to reveal something of His heart, mind, will, and purpose to the church. Not surprisingly, the enemy is using tactics to prevent those with prophetic giftings from receiving revelation in order to stop them from proclaiming. The result is similar to keeping an eagle earthbound. Instead of fulfillment and freedom, the prophet feels frustrated and restricted. Using the parallels between prophetic people and biblical references to eagles, Rodney Kingstone demonstrates the detrimental effect that earthbound eagles have on the church and how the body of Christ can be instrumental in seeing their own prophetic people soar once again.
ISBN 0-9785398-0-X $12.00 USD

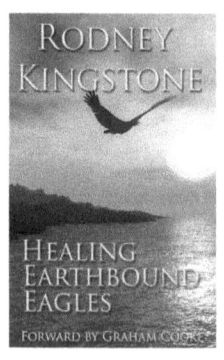

Visit www.LivingWordEvents.org
GoldenEaglePublishing/Books

Send checks to:
Golden Eagle Publishing
11413 W I-70 Frontage Road, North
Wheat Ridge, CO 80033
Call with a Credit Card: 303-989-2208

GOLDEN EAGLE SCHOOL OF MINISTRY

The purpose and intention of the school is to provide sound biblical and practical applications to various ministry disciplines within the local body. We endeavor to equip each student with the necessary instruction and applications to cause them to be an asset to their local body and the church at large. Our curriculum is designed to help the student hear God's voice more clearly through His written Word, the Voice of the Holy Spirit, and to build character through the practical application of doing the works of God. As part of that scenario, intimacy with God builds the personal relationship required for effective, powerful ministry in the body. This lays the foundation of the Word and the Spirit, not just imparting knowledge but building character through God working in each student. In this orchestration, the student becomes an embodiment of his or her ministry gift or calling.

On-site or off-site classes and seminars such as:

- Prophetic I & II – Hearing the Voice of God, Rich Harris, Instructor
  (Syllabus for Part I available in English, Spanish, and Russian)
- A Prophetic Look at the Hebraic Foundation of the Church I & II, Brooklyn Heaney, Instructor
  (Syllabus for Part I available in English, Spanish, and Russian)

All off-site seminars are custom tailored to suit the needs and time frame of the host ministry. They include a full syllabus and time for prophetic activation. All information concerning these classes and others may be found on our website under Golden Eagle School—Course Descriptions.

For more information:
Living Word Ministries International
and Golden Eagle School of Ministry
Rich Harris
303-989-2208
LivingWordEvents@gmail.com
www.LivingWordEvents.org

CPSIA information can be obtained
at www.ICGtesting.com
Printed in the USA
JSHW021219131122
33070JS00003B/89